✳ American Quilts ✳

BOOK 1: ELLEN's STORY

First Aladdin Paperbacks September 2000

Text copyright © 2000 by Susan E. Kirby

Aladdin Paperbacks
An imprint of Simon & Schuster
Children's Publishing Division
1230 Avenue of the Americas
New York, NY 10020

Printed and bound in the United States of America

10 9 8 7 6 5 4 3

Library of Congress Control Number 00-107117

ISBN: 0-689-80969-7

Love to Aunt Laurel and Uncle Eldy
You've given me such happy memories,
Giggles, and overnights with Julie
The walnut grove
The barn
Old Tony, who stepped on Rick's bare foot
Mad dashes to the Food Circus
Dinner at Streids and Barneys. Fancy-shmancy!
Uncle Eldy never once getting cross when we were a trial
And we were
Aunt Laurel taking the corners sharp, singing "A-Round the Corner!"
And correcting my grammar
Thank you for every golden stitch you put into my childhood

Acknowledgments

I'm grateful for the generosity of those who have shared their time and expertise in answering my many questions:

Marcia Lutz—Your family history came with perfect timing. I appreciate your friendly voice on the phone.

Lorraine O'Hern—Thank you for sharing your photos of the Hornbuckle Quilt. A picture truly _is_ worth a thousand words!

Joseph Edward Garrera, Historical Research and Writing— Your appraisal of the Hornbuckle Quilt underscores its historical significance.

Mary Ann Munyier—Curartor of Collection with New Salem—Your timely answers, insights, and enthusiasm for my project made research a pleasure.

Mark L. Johnson, Historic Sites Historian—You answered the elementary and the obscure and even provided illustrations!

The staff and volunteers at New Salem Village—Thank you for making learning fun as you share from your treasure trove of living history.

Mount Hope-Funks Grove Library and the Alliance Library System—Once more, your staff has faithfully accommodated me by tracking down reference books. Thank you!

Dear Reader:

Perhaps you have read of "Honest Abe" Lincoln walking six miles to rectify a six-and-a-quarter-cent error made to a woman while clerking at Offutt's Store in New Salem. Though the woman remains a mystery in history textbooks, it was commonly known in the New Salem community, and is verified by Hornbuckle descendents that Clarissa Hornbuckle was the woman Lincoln overcharged.

Clarissa and her husband, Washington, homesteaded three miles from New Salem. They were the parents of two daughters, Louisa and Areanna, and four sons. Thanks to the generosity of the Hornbuckle descendents, the blue-and-white Orange Peel quilt that Clarissa fashioned from the fabric she bought from Lincoln is on display at Lincoln's Salem State Historic Site south of Petersburg, Illinois. Louisa and Areanna's names, stitched into the border of the quilt all those years ago, are legible with the aid of a magnifying glass.

Ellen is a fictional character. But her father, Gil Tandy, is based loosely upon my great-great grandfather, Isaac Funk. A farmer and stockman, Isaac was recognized as a veteran of the Black Hawk War because he carried a message to his troops. The nature of the message he delivered is unknown. Family legend has it that Isaac periodically entrusted "banking responsibilities" to his young sons.

The winter of 1830–1831 went down in the history books of the heartland as the "Winter of the Deep Snow." In later years, "snowbirds" gathered at "Old Settler Reunions" and reminisced about the hardships that winter.

I hope my quilt series will make you curious about the lives and times of *your* ancestors and that you, too, will write a story.

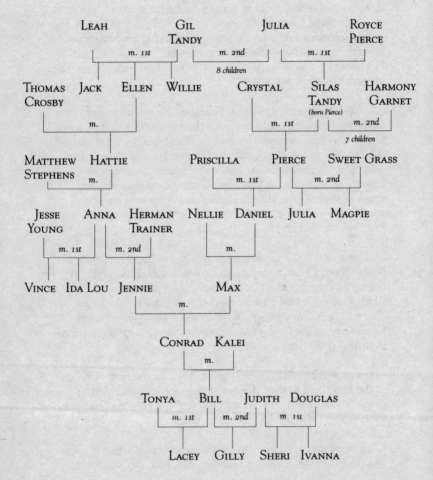

✳ **American Quilts** ✳

BOOK 1: ELLEN's STORY

✳ ✳ ✳ SUSAN E. KIRBY ✳ ✳ ✳

ALADDIN PAPERBACKS
NEW YORK   LONDON   TORONTO   SYDNEY   SINGAPORE

Prologue

Ten-year-old Lacey Tandy sprang out of her stepmother's warm car. Freezing rain stung her cheeks and tickled the back of her knees as she dashed along the stone walk leading to the old farmhouse. She bounded up the porch steps and flung the door wide.

"Gram?" Lacey scanned the cluttered front room with an eager glance.

The potted plants and family pictures and quilts spilled love and comfort over the scarred furniture and scuffed wooden floor. She could see into the parlor where Gram liked to quilt. Flames licked at a log in the fireplace. A lamp with a stained-glass shade cast cheery light onto a handsome table. But Gram's favorite chair was empty.

Judith followed Lacey inside, car keys jingling in her hand. "Your shoes are damp, Lacey," she said, closing the door.

Lacey slipped out of her sneakers. She gave each cotton sock a tug and slid across the floor. "Where's my gram?"

The kitchen door swung open. "Who goes there?"

"Me, myself, and I!" cried Lacey.

Gram answered Lacey's smile with one of her own. "Where are the rest of my girls?"

"Ivana has a piano lesson this morning, and Sheri went to breakfast with her basketball team," said Judith.

Gram untied her bibbed apron and winked at Lacey. "I guess it's just you and me, kiddo."

Goody! Ever since her father had married Judith six months before, Lacey had had to share everything from her bedroom to her favorite cold cereal. It was a treat to have Gram all to herself for the day.

Lacey flung her coat toward the hall tree and skated over the polished floor into her great-grandmother's embrace. "It's raining cats and dogs, Gram."

"Isn't it, though?" Gram's tightly permed hair tickled Lacey's cheek as she hugged her close. "I'm keeping an eye on the creek."

Lacey relished the scents of fresh-baked cookies and face powder as she returned Gram's kiss. "Maybe it will overflow the banks and I can stay until the water goes down."

"If it washes out the lane, you won't have much choice in the matter," said Gram.

"I'll be back for you soon, if it doesn't stop raining. You too, Jennie," said Judith. She waved good-bye and ducked out the door again.

"Your house hasn't ever been flooded, has it, Gram?" asked Lacey.

"No. But family legend has it that the water *did* reach the edge of the yard once when there was nothing here but a log cabin and a pole barn. That was in eighteen thirty-one, after the Winter of the Deep Snow."

"The deep snow?" echoed Lacey.

Gram nodded. "There's a quilt in the humpback wooden trunk that dates back to that long-ago winter. The blue one there on the sofa is a replica of another that was begun the following autumn." She cupped a hand to her ear, inclined her head in the direction of the old trunk, and said, "Hear that? They're talking to you now."

Storytelling quilts? Lacey giggled.

Gram laughed and scurried off to the kitchen. But Lacey lingered in the front parlor, admiring the quilts. Those made by Gram's own hand were draped over the sofa and chairs. Some, made years ago, were worn and tattered. There were more quilts on racks and even more upstairs, displayed on the beds.

But the humpback trunk in one corner of the parlor held the really old quilts. They had been fashioned by family members who had long since "gone to their Maker," as Gram put it.

Gram returned with cookies, a pot of hot chocolate, and two cups. She settled the tray on the coffee table. Lacey plopped down on the sofa beside her. The steamy scent of chocolate wafted from the cups as Gram filled them.

Lacey stirred marshmallows into her hot chocolate. "Are you going to tell me about the deep snow?" she asked.

Gram passed Lacey a napkin and a cookie. "Yes. And then someday, you can tell your children and grandchildren. That way, the story won't be lost."

"Maybe we should write it down, just in case."

"It takes more than books." Gram patted her chest. "The spark to a story is in the heart—one that cares to tell. And another heart to listen."

Lacey thought of the sparks that had flown that morning when Sheri had said, "All your great-grandmother talks about is her old dead relatives. B-o-o-r-i-n-g!"

"She's so old-fashioned!" chimed Ivana.

That wasn't true! Gram cooked in her microwave and kept a cellular phone in her car, didn't she? Lacey set her cup down, shoved the rest of her cookie into her mouth, and said around a mouthful of crumbs, "You're the most interesting person I know. I'm never going to forget any of your stories!"

"That's my girl," Gram said with a smile.

When they had finished their snack, Gram opened the old humpback trunk and withdrew a red and white quilt. Lacey traced the neat lines of stitches running through the pretty quilt. "It makes me think of red birds on snow."

"Cardinals in winter," said Gram. "That's a pretty picture, all right."

Lacey stroked the quilt. It didn't feel anything like the homespun linsey-woolsy coverlet tucked away in the trunk. She knew that in the early days on the Illinois frontier, where her ancestors had settled, there had been no nearby town, no country stores, no place to buy yard goods. So the women had made their own cloth.

"It's store-bought cloth, isn't it?" asked Lacey.

"Yes, it is."

Lacey picked up the blue and white quilt on the sofa. "This one's just like it except blue."

"I made that a couple of years ago to remind me of the original."

"What happened to the original?" asked Lacey.

"It's on display in a place forty miles south of here. Thousands and thousands of people visit this little village every year."

"Have I been there?" asked Lacey.

"Yes, a few years ago. It's where the fabric for the quilt was bought over one hundred and fifty years ago. The clerk who sold it later became very famous."

"Famous?" Lacey climbed up on the wood box near Gram's quilting frame. "Hmm. How about another clue?"

Gram's eyes twinkled. "How about I just tell the story instead?"

"Is this the story about my great-great-great-great-grandmother Ellen?" asked Lacey, counting on her fingers to get it right.

"Yes, and more. It's about families." Gram adjusted the light over her quilting frame. "Like quilts, families are pieced together over time. If care is taken, they become a thing of beauty."

Lacey hugged her knees and thought about her own "pieced" family. Dad and Judith, Ivana and Sheri and herself. Were they a thing of beauty? "Is it a happily ever after story?" she asked.

Gram chuckled. "That's only in fairy tales."

"I thought so." Lacey sighed.

"There's a big 'Me, Myself, and I' inside of everyone, Lacey. Turning that 'me' into 'we' wasn't any easier back then than it is now," said Gram. "It means being kind and patient and loving."

"Even when I don't feel like it?"

"*Especially* when you don't feel like it. It's like quilting. You work at it day in and day out, and you get something strong and lasting."

A log shifted on the fire. Embers sizzled and popped. Gram tunneled her needle through the quilt top, the batting, and the muslin backing. The thread whispered as she pulled it taut. The whispering sounded to Lacey like voices from the past.

Chapter One

May 1830

A playful breeze tangled Ellen Tandy's sunbonnet ties as she stooped, weeding the garden. Sweat matted a fringe of bark-colored hair to her forehead and stung her hazel eyes. "Ouch!" She plucked a pinching dirt clod from between her toes, then straightened to rest her back.

The Illinois prairie was covered in shin-high grass and wildflowers with patches of fresh-turned fields. Ellen scanned the landscape for some sign of Father, but without success. Was he at Aunt Clarissa's? Rarely did he go to Springfield without a side trip to Rock Creek, where his sister lived with her family. Ellen wished she could have gone, too. What fun it would be to see her cousin Louisa again!

Matilda, the goose, waddled into the garden and uprooted a tender pea vine. Ellen flapped her homespun skirt. "Scat, Matilda. Go find a bug."

Matilda squawked and flapped her wings and scuttled off to pester Ellen's brothers, Jack and Willie. They had helped Father with the plowing and harrowing and sowing. The oats were in the ground, as well as wheat and a little flax. The flax was for cloth making. Ellen wasn't sure she could make cloth without Mama to help her. But you didn't say "I can't" to Father. Instead, she'd asked him to bring her blue calico from Mr. Iles's store in Springfield.

"Shoo!" scolded Jack from the nearby field.

Ellen swung around to see Matilda snitching the corn the boys were planting before Willie could close the holes with his foot. Matilda hissed at Jack and tried to pinch his bare toes. He picked up a small dirt clod and pelted her with it.

"Aw, Jack. All she wants is a bite," said Willie. He was seven, and no match for the goose. He reached into the buckskin pouch that hung from his shoulder and lost another kernel of corn to Matilda.

"That's it for today, Willie. Get going, and take that pesky goose with you," said Jack. He was sixteen, and in charge while Father was gone.

Willie gave the seed pouch to Jack, then clambered over the split-rail fence into the prairie pasture where cattle grazed.

"Here, goosey, goosey. Willie's got corn," Willie coaxed Matilda along.

The goose chortled over the seed he tossed her. She squawked and flapped her wings and waddled after him, following a path in the grass. The path had been made by wildlife, then followed by Indians, and now by settlers like Father and their livestock. It was the path that would bring Father home. *When he came*.

Ellen was worried. 'Course, you didn't worry at her house, either. Not out loud. Or show your fear. Because if you did, Jack would tease.

"Are you about done?" Willie called to Ellen.

"Close enough," said Ellen.

"Let's go down to the creek, then."

Ellen picked up a stick at the edge of the garden and measured the depth of the ash barrel in passing. It would be up to her to make soap from those ashes. Soap from ashes, candles from tallow, flax to grow and rot and beat and spin and weave and sew. Crowded by the thought of it all, she flung the stick over the woodpile at the edge of the timber where the blackberry bushes grew and rushed headlong into the woods.

"Hey! Wait for me!" called Willie.

They stopped at the fallen log that spanned the swollen creek.

"Say we make a three-face camp," said Willie. "This'll be our plow." He reached for a forked limb. "Pretend I'm Father. I plant corn, then the Kickapoo Indians come. You can be Mama."

"Huh-uh. I'm Chief Machina." Ellen stripped a handful of green leaves from a nearby sapling and pretended to be the noble chief, upset over so many white families making their homes on the prairie. "Too much, too many. White man go before leaves fall," she ordered, and scattered her handful of leaves just as Chief Machina had done seven years earlier when Father had planted his first crop of corn.

Willie lapped his arms across his chest and spread his bare feet. "Machina must share the land with his white brothers now. He made treaty with Boss Hickory."

Boss Hickory was President Andrew "Old Hickory" Jackson. Ellen thrust out her chin, bristling over the insult of invading settlers. "Machina hand not on the feather."

"Doesn't matter who signed. Treaty can't be broken as long as the sun rises in the East."

Ellen scowled and scribbled in the air with her finger and made her voice sour: "White man quick, putting black on white."

"Yup," said Willie.

He said it so much like Father that, suddenly, their playacting touched too close to the reality of wandering bands of Indians and other dangers on the frontier. Springfield was a day's ride, and Father had been gone five. *What could be keeping him?*

Ellen turned away and wiped stinging eyes with hands that smelled like weeds. Crying was something else you didn't do. Or at least, you tried not to. She spit on her palms, rubbed them together, and kept walking.

Willie raced to catch up. "Where're you goin'?"

"Home."

"How come?"

Because worries, like weeds, weren't that easy to shake, once they took hold. Ellen tried to drive away scary thoughts with hopeful ones: "I hope Louisa comes home with Father."

Surprised, Willie asked, "Did you ask him to bring her?"

"No," admitted Ellen. She had *wanted* to ask. Had tried to, even as Father rode away. Maybe if he'd turned and looked back, she would have. But he didn't. Not even to wave. It made her shrink inside, standing there with her hand in the air and Father's thoughts so firmly fixed ahead that he had not looked back.

Had it been that way for Mama, too, when Father was away, buying steers from homesteaders far and near? Aunt Clarissa said it was a dangerous life. "I'd think you'd worry yourself sick!" Ellen remembered her saying to Mama. Mama had lifted her chin and said in that strong, quiet way of hers, "God knows where he is."

God knows, Ellen tried to comfort herself in Mama's confidence that God looked after His children, large and small. If they wanted to be looked after. But what if Father didn't? What if, someday, he just kept going and never came back?

That was the worst worry of all.

Chapter Two

As Ellen watched for Father, her cousin Louisa sat on a front yard stump, forty-five miles southwest, watching for him, too. She was hoping he would bring Ellen with him the way he used to do before Aunt Leah died.

"No, no, Areanna!" Louisa's red hair fell in her eyes as she jumped up to stop her little sister from poking a piece of corn in her nose. "Give me that."

Areanna, who was two, squealed in protest at Louisa's intervention. She followed her back to the stump, squalling for the ear of corn.

Louisa hid it in the hollowed middle of the stump, and sat down. "Sing with me," she cajoled, and made up a song as she plunked Areanna on her lap:

"There is a cat, her name is Ellen,
She likes juicy red watermelon.
She likes to nip and she likes to nap,
And she 'specially likes mouses that
climb on her lap."

On the last line, Louisa pretended to gobble Areanna up. Areanna laughed so hard she blew snot bubbles.

Louisa made a face. "Icky sticky. That's what you get for poking corn up your nose. Hold still!"

Louisa paused in wiping Areanna's nose to see a

horse galloping toward their cabin. *Uncle Gil?* She let go of Areanna and jumped up on the stump for a better look.

It was a boy coming. He sawed on the reins at the edge of the yard, and nearly flew over his horse's head. Eyes blazing, sweat streaming down a wintery white face, he shrieked, "A poison snake bit my father. He's going to die if he doesn't get a doctor quick!"

"New Salem's the closest! Three and a half miles north!"

"Would you run to the creek and tell my mother help's coming?"

He galloped away without waiting for an answer. Pulse bucking, Louisa grabbed Areanna and ran until she couldn't. Areanna was an armful to carry and too short to run. It seemed to take forever to reach the creek, one-half mile away. Louisa stumbled along the bank, dragging Areanna by the hand until she found the covered wagon.

A man lay motionless on the ground by the wagon. A woman knelt beside him, wiping his fevered brow. One glance sucked the breath out of Louisa. His foot was horribly swollen and discolored.

The woman gritted her teeth and gripped the front of his shirt. "Don't you leave us in the middle of nowhere, Boyce. Don't you dare!"

The man's chin slumped to his chest. Death rattled in his throat. The woman turned gray, grabbed his limp wrist, then beat on his chest and wailed.

Louisa stumbled over a log, backing away, and raced

home as fast as Areanna's short legs would allow. They passed the cabin without stopping and went on to the corn patch where her mother was hoeing.

"Mama! Mama! There's a woman down at the creek needs help! Her husband's . . . " Louisa couldn't make herself say the word. She burst into tears.

Mama tossed the hoe aside, cupped her hands to her mouth, and called to Louisa's father, who was working at the other end of the field.

The woman's name was Julia Pierce. The boy's name was Silas. Piecing their story together, Louisa's parents learned that Captain Pierce had been a military man. He had been assigned to a new post and was en route to the fort at Rock Island and was taking his family with him. That seemed odd to Mama. Of late, there'd been Indian trouble up that way.

"That's no place for women and children," Louisa heard her say.

Julia pressed her lips together and offered no explanation.

Louisa's father arranged the burial while Silas stumbled around in the yard, cracking a whip that had belonged to his father. Louisa was keeping her distance. It wasn't shyness. It was his sorrow. Instead of bawling his eyes out as could be expected, he crack, crack, cracked that whip until she wished she could hide it from him.

Instead, she crowded out the sound of it with a revised chant:

Ellen's Story

"There is a girl, her name is Ellen.
She likes juicy red watermelon.
She likes to sing and she likes to dance.
She'll come see her cousin if she gets the chance."

Louisa was shelling peas on the stump in the front yard when Uncle Gil rode up to the cabin the next day. He wasn't any bigger than Daddy, but he looked tall and tough in the saddle, with leathery skin and prominent cheekbones and piercing gray eyes. His sternness was a challenge to Louisa. She jumped up and used Mama's chiding voice, trying to win a smile: "Didn't I say bring Ellen next time?"

"'Afternoon, Louisa," said Uncle Gil, his mouth tipping enough to make her trouble worthwhile.

"Mama's been watching for you for a week or more."

"Got her sermon all ready, I reckon."

"She figured the rain would bring you," said Louisa. "Or didn't it rain up your way?"

"I thought it would never quit." Leather creaked as he swung out of the saddle, mud splattered and trail worn. He had his bull's tongue plowshares with him and a sack of milled corn.

"Looks like you have company."

Louisa glanced at the nearby covered wagon. "It's Julia and Silas. They were passing through when Captain Pierce got snakebit and died. Julia doesn't know what to do with herself."

"Mrs. Pierce to you, Lou, and tend your own knitting," said Louisa's father as he strode from the cabin to meet Uncle Gil. "Good to see you, Gil. How are things up your way?"

"Wet when I left," said Uncle Gil.

"Here, too," said Daddy, shaking Uncle Gil's hand.

Louisa grabbed her bowl of peas off the stump and ran inside. Mama was making soup from a couple of prairie hens Daddy had snared. She was stirring her kettle on the hearth and talking in short, hushed words to Julia. Louisa heard Uncle Gil's name mentioned before Mama swung around and saw her. "All done?"

Louisa gave her the bowl of shelled peas. "Uncle Gil's here."

"I know," said Mom. "Supper will be ready in a shake."

Mama's look said scoot. Curious over what it was she'd been saying to Julia, Louisa stalled. "Shall I tell the men to wash up?"

"Do that," said Mama. "Go on, now."

Louisa darted out the door to hear her father telling Uncle Gil the whole story about Captain Pierce.

"Buried him yesterday. Sad business," said Daddy. "Left his widow in a fix."

"Has she got family?"

"Back in Boston. The boy has grandparents in Cincinnati. But it's a long haul."

"And a hard road, for a woman and a boy traveling alone," agreed Uncle Gil. "If she could get to Springfield, she might find a storekeep going east for supplies. It'd make for a safer trip."

"I said the same thing. But Mrs. Pierce doesn't seem inclined to look to her in-laws for help."

"Why not?"

Daddy shrugged and shifted his feet. "Something about apples not falling far from the tree. Clarissa smells a rat somewhere."

"Not in the pie safe, I hope!" cried Louisa.

Daddy frowned at her. "You standing here for a reason?"

"Mama said wash up, supper's ready."

"Go call the boy, then," said Daddy. He took charge of Uncle Gil's horse. "There's water on the bench there, Gil. Wash up."

Louisa went around back where Silas was cracking his whip. He was as fair as Julia was dark. His eyes were gray, Julia's were blue. He moved like a hog crossing a frozen creek. Julia, she'd noticed, was surefooted and graceful.

"Supper's ready," said Louisa, then dashed around the cabin just in time to follow Uncle Gil inside.

He took off his hat and got it crushed as Mama jumped up and hugged him.

"Julia, this is my brother I've been telling you about," said Mama, turning to Julia. "Gil, I'd like you to meet Julia Pierce."

"Ma'am," said Uncle Gil.

Julia met his gaze and returned his nod. But something in her eyes made Louisa think of a cornered cat. Uncle Gil shifted his feet and slapped his hat against his leg. It was a soft sound, punctuating a lull in words. Mama soon filled it with chatter, asking about Ellen and the boys and the farm and Uncle Gil's trip to Springfield.

When grace was said, and the eating began, Uncle Gil mentioned that he was in the market for steers. Mr. Iles, he said, had sold his store and turned his attention to hotel keeping and banking. He had given Uncle Gil a loan to invest in more livestock.

"I've got some calves you can look at," said Daddy, and Uncle Gil nodded.

"Does Mr. Iles's replacement have any blue willow dishes in stock?" Mama asked Uncle Gil as he dipped corn dodgers in his soup.

"Blue, you say? Sorry, Clarissa. Can't say as I noticed."

Louisa lifted her wooden bowl. All winter, as Mama carded wool and made her spinning wheel fly, she'd talked of blue willow dishes. She guessed she'd have to see a blue willow to know if it was pretty or not.

"How many calves have you got?" asked Uncle Gil.

"Four, to part with. Thought I'd put a little more weight on them before I sell," said Daddy.

"Reckon we can come to terms. But it'll probably be early autumn before I get down this way again," said Uncle Gil.

"I could bring them to you," said Daddy. "How many head you planning on wintering?"

"Buying up whatever I can," said Uncle Gil.

"If you come up short on your corn crop, you could get pinched, feeding too many head over the winter," warned Louisa's father.

"There's risks to getting ahead," Uncle Gil replied.

"Ahead of what?" asked Mama in that chiding way she had with Uncle Gil. "Why, there's some who'd slit your throat on the chance you were carrying cattle gold in your pocket. Not to mention the Indians. The preacher's keeping us all posted on Black Hawk's quarrel with the squatters."

"Black Hawk's gone back to the west side of the river," said Uncle Gil.

"What about the Kickapoo?" challenged Mama.

"They've got nothing to do with it," inserted Louisa's father. "It's the Sac and Fox disputing an old treaty."

Mama sniffed. "Sac, Fox, Kickapoo—they all stick together."

Uncle Gil shook his head. "Not always, Clarissa. There's bad blood between some of them."

"Settlers can get caught in the middle of that, too!" said Mama. "Illinois will never be safe for children until the Indian problem is solved."

"Indians have children, too," reasoned Uncle Gil.

"You know what I mean!" Mama tilted her chin.

Abruptly, Julia left the table and the cabin. Silas followed.

Uncle Gil looked from their empty places to Mama's red face. "What's that all about?"

"I reckon we upset her, talking about Indians," said Mama. "It was because of the trouble with Black Hawk that her husband was ordered to the fort at Rock Island." Eyes narrowing, she added, "And you, wandering the countryside with your children home alone."

"The trouble's died down. It was a good piece north and no danger to us, anyway," said Uncle Gil.

"Danger comes in all shapes and sizes," retorted Mama. "Why, if the Indians hadn't got all riled up, Captain Pierce wouldn't have been traveling north. And if he hadn't been traveling, he'd have come nowhere near the snake that bit him."

"If, if," replied Uncle Gil. "It's a slothful man worries over a lion in the street."

"And a fool who ignores one," replied Mama.

"Lions?" asked Louisa, alarmed. "In Springfield?"

Daddy and Uncle Gil exchanged a glance and burst out laughing. Even Mama had a hard time keeping her mouth straight.

"Your uncle's quoting a proverb," explained Mama.

Louisa wiped her mouth and said, "I knew that."

After supper, Louisa helped Mama tidy up, then went outside to pick violets under the tree in the backyard. Uncle Gil and Mama paid her no heed as they came out for a stroll.

"Trusting Jack to look after the farm while you're off buying livestock is one thing," Mama said, taking him to task. "But leaving Ellen and Willie with him is another. They are too young to be without an adult when you're away so much."

"I haven't got much choice."

"You *do* have a choice, and you're making it every time you ride away," argued Mama. "Nothing against your ambitions, mind you. Wash is looking to buy more land, too. But you won't catch him rambling over the countryside, trading in livestock to do it."

"What's this about blue willow dishes?"

"I'm comparing prices, is all. I can get them any time I want, so don't you get uppity with me, Gil Tandy."

"You can meddle in my affairs, but I can't ask you about dishes?"

"We're not talking about me, we're talking about you leaving your children alone," said Mama. "If you're going to make these trips, then you need a wife to look after the children and keep the cabin."

"You mean Mrs. Pierce?" asked Uncle Gil.

"Yes," said Mama.

Uncle Gil's upper lip stretched tighter, leaner. "This your idea or hers?"

"Mine. But I mentioned it to her, and she didn't bolt and run."

Uncle Gil leaned against the tree trunk, shoulders bunched. "What'd she say?"

"She's willing to try it out."

"Try it out? You don't put your hand to the plow and look back."

"She doesn't see it that way."

"If she decides it isn't working out? What then?"

"She'll open a millinery in Springfield."

"What's a millry?" asked Louisa.

Mama turned and frowned at her. "Hush, Louisa, and go find your sister."

Chapter Three

Julia Pierce lay flat on the floor of the wagon, too empty to pray and long past tears. Silas was out behind the barn. His whip cracking the air sent her thoughts reeling back three days, to the beginning of the end.

It had been an awful day. The green flies had driven the horses half mad, drawing blood with their bites. The poor brutes would have run away with the wagon had the mud not been so deep, the pulling so hard. They got stuck twice in the morning. Frustration drove Boyce to the bottle. The second time they got stuck, they had to empty the wagon of all but bare necessities. By brute strength and sheer cussedness, Boyce pried the mud-locked wagon wheels free. Julia assumed he would reload the furniture. When he didn't, she spoke up.

"Abandon everything? You can't be serious?"

"We're only a couple of days from the post," Boyce replied with a thrust of his chin.

"But what will we sleep on? How will we set up housekeeping when we get there? My quilts. My dishes. My . . ."

"Your what?" Boyce cut her short. "Look at those horses! You're killing them, taking the east, west. Leave it go! Leave it all go! Throw out that god-awful teapot, too. If you won't, I will!"

He would have, too, except Silas beat him to it. The teapot was a gift from Julia's mother, and all she had left of her. But there was no reasoning with Boyce when he was drinking.

They were all exhausted by the time they made camp. Boyce told Julia to clean the mud off herself before starting supper. He knew she hated mud. She thought that his anger was spent, and left him unhitching the team while Silas gathered firewood.

The cold bath in the creek revived her cautious optimism. Boyce's head would clear by morning. He would see reason and go back for her trunks of dishes and linens and household goods. Then she heard raised voices.

Julia's heart reeled to that familiar black corner as she scrambled up the bank and over the soppy ground to find Boyce hunkered down, shouting at Silas cowering under the wagon.

"What am I raising here? A soldier or a mama's boy?"

"Stop it!" she pleaded. "Leave him alone, you're not yourself."

"Stay out of it!" warned Boyce.

"Please, Boyce. You're scaring him."

"It's you, not me!" he roared. "You're ruining him like you ruin everything!"

Julia froze at Silas's stricken face, and her teapot clutched in his arms. *Oh, Silas!*

"I hid it," she shrieked to draw his anger away from Silas. "It wasn't him, it was me! Leave it, Silas. Go on down to the creek and bathe. Go on!"

The next moment was blurred in her mind. Silas squealed and rolled toward the far side as Boyce's whip sang. Julia screamed and caught his arm. Boyce cursed and fell forward as he tried to shake her off. Julia fell with him. On her way down, she saw the snake poised to strike.

And the snake bit him.

Boyce died. Slowly. Painfully, swearing to the last that the snake, not Silas, had been his target.

His whip had not cut Silas, Julia told herself as they put Boyce in the ground. And again when Silas asked to keep the whip and she let him. And yet again, when each crack of that whip held up a mirror to her failed marriage, her feeble mothering, and a broken boy.

For lack of options, she would marry Mr. Tandy if he agreed to her conditions: He must retrieve her belongings from the roadside where Boyce had abandoned them, and he must never lay a hand on Silas.

Chapter Four

Ellen climbed Lookout Point, a low bluff at the edge of the timber. Willie scrambled up the trail and plunked down beside her.

"Look!" he said, holding a short stick to his eye as if it were a seaman's telescope. "A sailing ship!"

"Is not," said Ellen.

Father was days overdue. Ellen was in no mood for pretending. Her eyes watered from scanning the sunny horizon.

"Something, though. Way out there," said Willie, pointing.

Occasional groves of trees made dark blotches on the grassy landscape. A speck Ellen hadn't seen before grew into a wagon and team.

"It's Father!" cried Willie.

"It can't be," said Ellen. "Father doesn't have a covered wagon."

"Look at the horse! Not the team, the horse *behind* the wagon!"

The horse *did* look like Father's mare, Gertie. Ellen's pulse quickened.

"He's waving his hat! See? I told you it was Father!" Willie jumped up and waved both arms.

"But who is that with him?" asked Ellen. There was

a woman on the wagon seat beside Father and a third person riding Gertie and driving along half a dozen young steers.

"Can't tell from here. Race you!" Willie dropped over the edge of the bluff and skidded along on his bottom.

Excited at the prospect of company, Ellen was about to follow when she snagged her homespun skirt on a thorny bush. She stopped to untangle her skirt and hollered after Willie, "I'm not racing, Willie."

"Are, too. I called it."

"But I didn't agree," argued Ellen. She started down the bluff after him.

"It's still a race."

"Is not!"

"Is snot, is snot," chanted Willie, giggling. "Yikes! Snake!" He pulled up short, grabbed the nearest sapling, hoisted himself into it, and clamped his thin legs around the skinny trunk while Ellen hastily retreated to the top of the bluff.

At the same moment, Father was swinging to the ground at the foot of the bluff. He reached under the wagon seat for his gun. "Is it a rattler, Willie?"

"Rattler?" It was a boy riding Father's horse. The steers scattered as he exploded out of the saddle with a stockman's whip in hand. "I'll kill it! Let me kill it!"

"No, Silas!" cried the woman. She gathered her long skirts and started to scramble out of the wagon.

"Stay put!" Father warned. "You, too, Silas."

The boy charged up the bluff like he hadn't heard.

"Where is it? Where's the rattler?"

"There! In the grass." Willie pointed with one hand and clung to the tree with the other. "Could be just a . . ."

Willie's last words were lost as the boy cracked his whip. The rawhide cord sizzled through the air. It popped like lightning as it struck a young tree. Severed leaves flew every which way.

"There it goes!" cried Willie.

Ellen's skin crawled at the sight of the snake slithering over a bald spot on the steep bluff. The woman on the wagon seat below saw it, too. She was on her feet again, terror in her voice. "Get away from there, Silas! Get away I say!"

Silas took aim on the snake. He cracked his whip, and missed. The rawhide strands wrapped around the branches of a bush. He tugged and pulled and jerked so hard, his toed-in feet flew out from beneath him. The woman screamed as he squealed and scrambled sideways to avoid falling on top of the snake.

"It's a . . . wh-o-o-a!" he cried.

The whip broke free, taking the bush and Silas with it. His outcry echoed as he toppled down the bluff, clutching at clumps of grass and brambles and weeds. He bumped over tree roots and tore up the sod with his dragging heels and rolled right into the wagon wheel. " . . . big 'un." The impact with the wheel jolted the last two words out of Silas.

The woman slumped back onto the wagon seat and buried her pale face in her hands.

Willie dropped out of the sapling. He slid down the

bluff, chattering. "What took you so long? Ground's dry and we've been planting. Ellen was hoping you'd bring Louisa."

"Was it a rattler?" blurted Ellen.

"No," said Willie. "Just an old bull snake."

Father fixed Silas with a narrowed eye. "Snakes are thicker than flies around here. Some are harmless, but others can kill you."

"Not if I kill them first," said Silas, shaking himself off.

Ellen saw Father's jaw tighten and his eyes flash. She sucked in her breath as the woman piled off the wagon and gripped the boy by the shoulder.

"You listen to Mr. Tandy, Silas!" she said. Her shrillness was gone, but there was ownership in her hands.

Father swallowed whatever he was going to say and returned his gun to the wagon. Ellen couldn't take her eyes off the woman. She was almost as tall as Father, but milky pale. Dark hair fringed her bonnet. Her eyes were the color of blue violets and so was her dress. Ellen had never seen anything so soft and pretty as that blue dress or the woman wearing it.

"You must be Willie," said Silas, breaking away from his mother's trembling grip. "You sure do know your way up a tree."

Willie shuffled his feet and tugged at his bottom lip.

"Ellen, Willie," said Father. "This is Silas Pierce and his mother, Julia." Father knelt down and beckoned Ellen and Willie closer. "They'll be staying from here on out," he said. "Julia and I got married yesterday."

Ellen's Story

The shock of it was like stepping off the tailboard of a wagon into black space. "Married?" squeaked Ellen.

Father nodded.

Julia's petal-soft dress blurred before Ellen's eyes. She pinched a piece of her own faded butternut-colored dress and remembered her mother's rough hands weaving the homespun fabric. She lifted her face. "But, why?"

Father's mouth stretched even thinner. "A girl needs a mother, Ellie. Willie, too."

A *mother*? She asked for calico and he brought her a mother?

Chapter Five

Father handed Julia up on the wagon seat. He moved to lift Ellen up to sit beside her. But Ellen stepped out of reach.

"You can ride with me if you want," said Silas. He swung aboard Gertie, then leaned out of the saddle and stretched a hand down to Ellen.

He was less gawky looking in the saddle with his long legs in the stirrups. And still, Ellen declined. Silas made the same offer to Willie. To Ellen's surprise, Willie accepted.

"You sure, Ellie? There's room," said Willie, giving her a second chance to climb up, too.

"I'm walking," she said shortly, falling in step behind the wagon.

"Round up those steers and drive them on up to the house," Father called after the boys.

But Silas and Willie were already thundering away on Gertie. When the sound of her hooves faded, Ellen could hear Father talking to the team. Or was he talking to Julia? *His new wife.*

Was this her fault? Had Father married Julia because he thought she needed a mother? Someone who could do the many tasks she hadn't yet mastered?

Ellen neared the homestead to see Silas walking

Gertie to the pole barn. Willie was racing across the cornfield where Jack stood staring at the newcomers. Matilda chased after him, squawking and flapping her wings.

Father drove the wagon right up to the cabin door and helped Julia down. Ellen dodged a thistle in the grass and crossed the freshly sown field to join her brothers.

"Willie's havin' a little fun. Says Father got married," said Jack. His mouth tilted as if to say he wasn't about to be taken in by a joke like that.

"It's true."

Jack's grin faded. His eyes were hazel like hers and Mama's. He had Mama's big-boned frame, too, and her practical temperament. But the long upper lip, broad nose, and high brow were replicas of Father's. "You two have had your fun. Now who are they, really?"

"Go ask Father if you don't believe us," said Ellen.

Jack looked toward the cabin where Father was carrying a trunk into their cabin. He hunkered down on the ground without saying a word and rested his forearms on his knees, his weight balanced on the balls of his feet.

Ellen wished Jack would say something. She dragged her fist over her smarting eyes and blurted, "All I wanted was blue calico."

Jack picked up a dirt clod and rolled it between his work-toughened palms. "No use cryin' over spilt milk, Ellie."

Ellen shook off the dirt he sprinkled over her toes,

breaking up the dirt clod. Something inside her was breaking apart, too.

"What should we do?" asked Willie, running a hand over Matilda's sleek back, smoothing feathers.

"I dunno. Maybe it'll be all right," Jack said with a shrug. "She's bound to be a better cook than Ellie."

"I can cook!" cried Ellen, glowering. "Good enough for the likes of *you*, anyway."

"Simmer down and use your head, Ellie," said Jack, catching her kicking foot in one broad calloused hand. "A family man can't get by on the frontier without a woman to hold the house together."

Struggling to free herself, Ellen bellowed, "Let go of my foot!"

"Say you're sorry for kickin'."

"I'm not a bit sorry! You're the one ought to be sorry!"

Ellen balanced herself on one foot and tried to jerk the other one free. But Jack tickled her toes and teased the way he always did when she lost her temper: "Say it, Ellie. Say it quick and I'll let go."

Willie moved away from Matilda to wiggle between them.

"You wantin' some of it, too?" Jack grabbed Willie's foot and jerked, pulling them both to the ground. Ellen swung at Jack with open palms.

"That does it! It's a fight to the finish," he teased.

Ellen squealed, for he nearly squeezed the life out of her. Play wrestling was as close to hugging as Jack ever got. There wasn't much dignity to it. But it melted

Ellen's anger. She hugged him back in the same wrestling fashion.

Jack caught Willie between his legs and tickled him with his bare toes. Willie broke free, then lunged at Jack, crying, "I'll save you, Ellie! I've got him. Break loose!"

Ellen rolled away and climbed to her feet. Willie looked no bigger than a gnat on Jack's broad chest. But he squawked and hollered like Indiana pigeons.

"You're pinned, Jack. I win!"

"It was those corn dodgers of Ellie's weighing me down," claimed Jack. He grinned at Ellen, clutched his belly, and moaned.

"I thought you boys planted this field."

Ellen's nerves jumped as she turned to see Father standing right behind her. Jack quit clowning around and rolled to his feet, bringing Willie up with him. "Got a good start, anyway."

"How's it supposed to grow with you rolling around, packing it down?" asked Father.

Jack shifted his weight and brushed himself off and leveled Father a glance. "Willie says you got married."

"That's right." Father slapped his hat against his leg and looked over the field and the stack of rails Jack had split while he was gone. "Having someone to keep the cabin will make things easier on all of us. Do your parts and show her the manners your mama taught you and I reckon things will go all right." He looked over his shoulder to the barn lot where Silas was flicking at flies with his whip and added, "Make the boy welcome, too."

"Can he work?" asked Jack.

"I don't know," said Father. "His father was a soldier, and durned if the boy doesn't seem bent on making war on snakes."

"We could do with a few less snakes around here," said Jack.

"Yup," said Father. Abruptly, he changed the subject. "I brought a few steers back with me. The boy scattered them back by the bluff. Round them up, Jack."

Jack nodded and said to Willie, "You coming, partner?"

Willie beamed and trotted after him. Matilda would have followed, too, but Father swung his hat at her and shooed her back toward the house.

"I'll send the boy," Father called after Jack. "But watch that whip of his. I don't want him putting marks on those steers."

Ellen fell in step with her father as he started toward the barn. She asked, "Was it a rattlesnake got Silas's father?"

"Yup, and don't you be asking any questions about it, either," he warned.

Ellen noticed his firmly set mouth and held back her questions about his new wife. She asked instead, "Did you get blue calico?"

"It slipped my mind, Ellie," he said. "It will have to wait until next trip."

Next trip. He just got back, and already he was thinking ahead to when he would leave again. Father touched her shoulder. The brush of his hand quickly turned into a nudge.

"Go see if Julia needs some help," he said.

What if I don't like her? What if she doesn't like me?
The words stuck in her throat.

Ellen reached the cabin on dragging steps and
closed the door behind her to keep Matilda from wad-
dling inside after her. She peered in at the trunks and
crates and boxes Father had already carried inside. Julia
lowered the lid to the trunk she was kneeling before,
and came to her feet Her lips relaxed, but it wasn't a
smile.

Disheveled and hot and cross that she should feel as
if she needed an excuse to enter her own home, Ellen
said, "The boys have planted corn all day. They'll be
wanting to eat soon."

"Is supper planned?" asked Julia. "Or should I take
care of it?"

"You can if you want to."

Julia nodded, then indicated her belongings with a
sweep of her hand. "I'm not sure where to put things.
There's more to carry in. Maybe you could help me
make room."

Ellen looked from her dust-spackled feet to Mama's
homemade loom and spinning wheel. They'd been
crowded against the wall to make room for Julia's
belongings. Her gaze flicked to the trundle bed and rum-
pled homespun coverlet Willie had crawled from
beneath that morning. "I could push the trundle bed
under," she offered grudgingly.

"Thank you," said Julia. She fit a white day cap over

her dark hair and turned to Ellen again. "Your cousin Louisa sent you a message. I think she slipped it into one of the trunks. It should be right on top," she said, going back out to the wagon.

It took only a moment to tidy the covers and push the bed in place. Ellen lifted the lid to the first trunk. Lying on top of quilts and linens was a tintype of a man in a soldier's uniform and Julia. She forgot the note for a moment and picked up the picture. The soldier was very handsome. He stood behind Julia, his hand resting on her shoulder. The fabric was wrinkled from the man's grip. But her mouth was sweetly held, so maybe his firm hand made her feel safe.

Ellen opened the second trunk. It was filled with clothing and dishes and household goods. If there was a note from Louisa, she couldn't find it. Father's boots scraped the puncheon floor. Ellen turned as he hauled in a lap-size writing desk. Julia followed, carrying something wrapped in muslin.

"That will be enough until we've seen what the cabin will hold," she said, and unwrapped a teapot from the cloth. The teapot was white, with a pine branch painted on the front. The spout, the handle, the rim, and the lid were decorated with delicate gold lines. Gently cradling it with both hands, she said to Father, "You may leave the wagon in the yard beside the cabin, please."

Father looked from the dainty teapot in Julia's possessive hands to her face. He shifted his feet. "I should have warned you it was just a pole cabin."

"The cabin is fine. You can leave the overflow in the wagon, along with the feather tick. I've grown used to sleeping there."

"And when the snow flies?"

"Let's take it a day at a time, Mr. Tandy."

Father was better at giving orders than taking them. But he banked the glint in his eye and crimped his hat and lowered his out-thrust chin. "I'll put a room on, as soon as I get time."

Julia acknowledged the offer with a mute nod.

"If there's anything else that needs saying, speak up."

"Silas is a good boy, but he's not a farm boy. You'll have to be clear in your directions, and patient if you want his help."

"Patience isn't my long suit," Father said plainly.

"I've noticed. I'm hoping you'll work on it."

Father made no reply.

"I'll not stand for him being a casualty of our agreement, Mr. Tandy."

"I don't know what you mean."

"I told you at Rock Creek. You're not to be harsh with him," Julia said. "If he tries your temper, leave him to me."

"Discipline is a tool, just like a hoe," replied Father. "Without it, you've soon got yourself a crop of weeds."

"There is discipline in grief."

"It won't teach him to plow."

"Neither will you, if you can't show restraint."

The lid of the trunk slipped from Ellen's sweaty hands and fell back, bumping the headboard of a bed

Father had carried in. It crashed to the floor before Ellen could catch it. Father and Julia both turned. Ellen's heart jumped at the spark that leaped to Father's eye.

"Have you been poking around where you've got no business, Ellen?"

"She's looking for Louisa's note," Julia said in the same voice she had used in speaking up for her son. "I told her she could."

Father's jaw got even tighter.

Julia turned her back on him. "Did you find it?" she asked Ellen.

Ellen shook her head.

"I'll look in the desk."

Father walked out while Julia was searching. She retrieved a scrap of paper from the writing desk he had carried in and gave it to Ellen.

Ellen's reading had gotten rusty since Mama died. Her eyes stumbled over the words written in elderberry juice. She held the note to her face, smelled it, pictured Louisa's fingers gripping the goose feather, her tongue flicking to the corner of her mouth, red hair falling over her face as she formed the letters with studied effort.

"You don't read?"

Ellen's skin flashed hot. She hung her head and mumbled, "Isn't anything to practice on, except Mama's Bible. The words are too hard."

Julia's fingers brushed Ellen's as she retrieved the note. Without further comment, she read it out loud:

"I have a cousin, her name is Ellen.
She likes juicy red watermelon.

She likes to sing and she likes to dance.
She'll come see her cousin if she gets the chance."

A poem about her! With rhyming words! For a moment, Ellen forgot her shame and anger at having to admit she could not read. Like butter melting over flapjacks, the warmth spilled over into a smile she couldn't hold back. She flushed again, and murmured, "Louisa's fun."

"She said the same thing about you."

"She did?"

Julia nodded and pressed the note into Ellen's hand. To look at her, Ellen doubted that she had much heart for fun. Must have some grit, though, standing up to Father. Or maybe she hadn't found out yet how flinty he could be. What'd they marry for, anyway?

Hours later, Ellen stretched out on her slab bed beneath Mama's old coverlet, still wondering. She thought about the tintype in Julia's blanket chest and about Julia having her wagon as her own personal room.

Did grown-ups ever playact? Like her and Willie, down by the creek, pretending to be Father and Machina. That's how Father's new marriage felt to her. A game of pretend where Mama was crowded out the same way Julia's trunks and crates and pretty things crowded their cabin.

Chapter Six

In coming days, Father and Jack felled and dragged logs into the yard for Julia's new room. They made good seats when the circuit preacher showed up on the second Wednesday in May. Twenty-one people gathered in their yard to hear young Reverend Crissey. Those who had come for a gander at Julia had to wait until after the sermon. Julia didn't come out of the cabin until the preaching started.

Mrs. Kelly made friends with her afterward. She had been Mama's friend, too, and Mr. Kelly drove stock with Father sometimes. Father invited them to stay for lunch. Reverend Crisswell stayed, too. He passed along news of the other settlements on his circuit. After lunch, he rode on. The men and boys went to the woods to fell more logs while Julia made tea.

Ellen peeked into the pot as it steeped. The brew was dark, instead of green or weak brown like the root and bark teas Mama used to make.

"How long has it been since ye left Boston, Mrs. Tandy?" asked Mrs. Kelly.

"Thirteen years," said Julia as she poured.

"'Tis my third year on the prairie," said Mrs. Kelly. "I miss the ocean's roar."

Ellen knew little about oceans and had even less

interest in Boston. But the lump of maple sugar Julia gave her for sweetening was generous beyond words.

"'Tis a gift to sit and drink tea like a lady again," said Mrs. Kelly. "Me sisters were but girls when they joined me in America. I had come ahead, and saved for their passage. The grandeur went right to their heads. Saucy lasses!"

Ellen tried to curl her little finger the way Mrs. Kelly's was curled as she sipped.

"While the household lay sleepin', me sisters brewed tea in games of pampered misses and handsome blue bloods comin' to call. And me, scoldin' and strivin' so to shape them into Beacon Hill domestics."

Julia's smiling lips curved over the rim of the cup in response to Mrs. Kelly's pert grin.

"We'd best be going, Annalee," called Mr. Kelly through the open window. "There's Daisy to milk, and chorin' to do."

"Ah, the life of spoiled lasses!" Mrs. Kelly said with a twinkle. She hugged Ellen and thanked Julia for her hospitality. "Your listenin' ears have been as good a tonic as the tea. Come see me, won't you, madear? And if it isn't askin' too much, would ye bring the wee teapot? We'll sit at me table, close our eyes, and pretend the wind moving over through the grass is a sea breeze."

The teapot's sprig of green and delicate twin pinecones made Ellen think of deep woods, not sea. But when Mrs. Kelly had gone, Julia lifted the lid and gazed inside as if it held the ocean's roar.

Ellen's arms ached from jogging the dash up and down. She pointed out the butter that was forming on the handle. "It's almost there. See?"

"I'll finish churning," said Julia. "You're free to go."

Father was gone to Rock Island to see a man at the fort about providing beef for the troops quartered there. He was not expected back until tomorrow, so when Julia said Ellen was free to go, she really *was* free. Ellen grabbed her sunbonnet, raced out the door, and skipped past stacks of logs in the yard.

In addition to field work, Father and Jack had peeled the bark and squared off most of the logs over the past few weeks. Once the notching was done, they would raise the walls. There was no hurry. But when Julia's room was done, it would be nicer than the cabin, which had started as a three-faced camp that Father closed in.

"Are you done already?" asked Willie. He was picking up the smaller limbs and sticks left from Father and Jack's log work.

"Julia's finishing," said Ellen. "Let's go to the creek."

"Wait'll I close Matilda into the barn."

"She can come, too," said Ellen.

"Huh-uh," said Willie. "Didn't you hear them last night?"

"The wolves?" asked Ellen, and he nodded.

Wolves were an ever-present danger, and not just for Matilda. Only recently had Father replaced the sheep they had killed last winter. With Matilda safely in the barn, Ellen and Willie darted into the green shade and birdsong of the shadowy woods. They raced to the crossing log that spanned the creek.

"Pretend we're going west," said Willie.

"We always go west."

"East, then," said Willie. He swung a leg to straddle the log, pretending it was a canoe. "We see pirates."

"I'll be a pirate." Ellen's bare feet gripped the log as she rose to tear a leaf from a low-hanging branch. Using her bonnet strings, she tied the leaf over her eye like a patch. "I'm Dead-Eye, the pirate!" She took a fighting stance with a flourish of her invisible sword.

"Pretend I sink your boat," said Willie.

"Huh-uh!" said Ellen. "Nobody sinks Dead-Eye's ship."

"We could build a raft," Silas spoke up from the bank.

Ellen frowned at the intrusion and turned to see him slapping his coiled whip against his leg.

"A real raft? One that would float?" asked Willie. "How?"

"Easy," said Silas. "We'll tie some logs together."

"Who's going to cut the logs?" asked Willie.

"They're already cut. Come on. I'll show you."

Ellen's eye twitched as Willie abandoned their game to trot after Silas. Over the past month, she had come to appreciate a few things about Julia, even if she wasn't making any effort to keep Father at home. But Silas was a different matter. She flicked a bug off the log and called to him, saying, "Didn't Jack tell you to take Milkweed to graze?"

"I am. She's just beyond the trees."

"You're supposed to watch her so she doesn't get into poison weed," said Ellen.

"If I don't know which weed is poison, what good does it do to watch?" reasoned Silas.

"Milkweed'll be all right. Let's go see about that raft," said Willie. "You coming, Ellie?"

Ellen struggled between principle and the lure of a raft. "I guess. If you want me to."

Silas shrugged. Ellen tossed her green patch aside and ambled after the boys, swinging her sunbonnet and splashing in the creek. The water was shallow and clear at the edges. It cooled her bare feet.

The logs Silas showed them turned out to be trees felled by beavers in the building of a dam. The ambitious beavers hadn't used all of the trees they had cut.

"See?" said Silas, nudging one of the leftover logs with his foot. "Our work's all done."

"Done? The logs are all different lengths," said Ellen.

"So? It won't be hard to cut them to one size," said Silas.

"And cut off the branches," said Willie.

"Any ideas how we can tie the logs together?" asked Silas.

"Grapevines, of course," said Ellen.

"Guess that'd work," said Silas. "What about an ax?"

"I'll get it," said Willie. He raced away and was back in short order with Father's ax.

Throughout the afternoon, Ellen took turns with

Willie and Silas, preparing the logs. All three of them wore blisters on their hands. Silas waded through a patch of poison ivy that Ellen had pointed out twice. He also smashed his thumb between two logs. But injuries aside, they made good progress. By suppertime, the logs were lined up on the bank, ready to be tied together.

Ellen's stomach rumbled as they left the woods and walked out onto the prairie where Milkweed was grazing. She stopped short when she saw what the cow was eating.

"Wild onions," said Willie.

Alarm pinched Silas's mouth. "Are they poison?"

"No, but they'll make her milk taste bad," said Willie.

"Shoo-ew!" said Silas, whisking his hand over his brow. "There for a minute, I thought we were in trouble."

"We?" echoed Ellen. "You're the one supposed to be watching her. When Father comes home, he'll taste the onion in the milk, and he'll know you weren't."

"What're you going to do?" asked Willie.

Silas reached down to scratch his ankle. "Suppose Milkweed were to kick her bucket?"

"Spill the milk, you mean?" asked Willie, and Silas nodded.

Ellen snorted. Milkweed wasn't that kind of cow. "Why don't you just *drop* the bucket, Silas. We'd all believe that."

Willie frowned at her. She broke a twig into pieces, flung it at both of them, and walked on to the cabin alone.

Ellen was setting the table when Silas came inside with Willie at his heels. "Want to help me, Willie?" she said.

"Can't," said Willie. "I'm showing Silas how I write my name, just as soon as we tell Julia about Milkweed."

"What about Milkweed?" asked Julia, looking up at them, her face flushed from the heat of the hearth.

Ellen waited for Silas to trip himself up in his yarn. But Julia didn't even question his kicked-the-bucket story, and Jack just went right on oiling his gun. Ellen couldn't believe it! She set the water bucket on the table and watched with a narrowed eye as Silas took the stick of charred firewood from Willie and wrote on the floor.

Willie pinched his chin and frowned. "Thought it was two dotted half sticks and one whole. Right, Ellie?"

"Those are *i*'s and *l*'s and there's two of each," said Silas. "See?"

"Two of each, huh? Ellie had it wrong."

"Did not." Certain she was right, Ellen asked, "Julia? How many *l*'s is there in Willie?"

"Two. Remember?" said Julia. She'd been giving Ellen reading and writing lessons as time allowed.

"Like this." Silas shifted position so Ellen could see as he wrote it again.

Ellen sniffed. "Water all right with you, Jack? For supper, I mean?"

Jack lifted his head. "Water?"

"Since there's no *milk*," she emphasized.

"Not going to be any wool, either, if we're not careful," he replied. "The wolves have sniffed out the sheep."

"Is that what all the ruckus was about last night?" asked Julia.

"There's wiggletails on the water," inserted Ellen, peering into the bucket.

"Tee stopped by while I was in the west field," said Jack.

Tee was the son of a neighbor and Jack's good friend. He was nearly as accident-prone as Silas. Ellen turned her head and listened.

"His mama lost a couple of geese to the wolves last week," Jack was saying.

"What if they come after Matilda?" asked Willie.

"We'll have us a nice crop of feathers," said Jack.

"Jack's teasing," soothed Julia. "He isn't going to let the wolves get Matilda. Tell him, Jack."

"That's one thing about milk," interrupted Ellen. "You don't have to strain out the wiggletails."

"Tell him what you and Tee plan to do, Jack," Julia prodded.

"I was thinking we'd slip the sheep out of the pen and trap the wolves there when they come looking." Jack stroked his long upper lip and let the silence stretch. He jerked his head in Silas's direction, and added, "Then we'll get the boy here to whip 'em right smart."

"Whip them?" said Silas.

"Now I know you're partial to snake whipping,"

drawled Jack. "But if Tee and me were to tie rattles on their tails, you could stir yourself to whip 'em, couldn't you?"

"I guess so," said Silas, starting to grin. "So long as I get to watch you tie the rattles on."

"Yah, Jack," Willie chimed in, snickering. "Let's see you tie the rattles on."

Jack flashed his warning grin. "You forget who's head of the pack, did you?"

"Father?" said Willie, eyes dancing.

"Try again, tadpole!" Jack leaped up and caught Willie in a headlock and tickled him to the floor.

Willie wiggled and giggled and squealed, "Julia!"

"Nope, it's not Julia. One more try," said Jack, holding him down with one knee and tickling him with both hands. "Who's head of the pack? Say it quick."

"Help me!" squealed Willie, in conniptions of giggles. "Silas! Help! Help!"

Silas piled on and got his head rubbed raw by Jack's knuckles and his legs whacked with the broom by his mother. Ellen wasn't partial to either treatment. And still, she felt edged out.

"No fighting in the house," said Julia, swinging the broom indiscriminately. "You boys quit, before you break something. Right now, or you can forget about supper!"

The boys untangled themselves and trooped to the table, ruddy cheeked and boisterous.

"One time Tee and me went on a ring hunt," Jack launched into one of his One-Time-Tee stories. "Every man in the neighborhood was there. Flushed out twenty-seven wolves. Tee got so excited, he fell off his horse in the midst of milling men and wolves and dogs. Afterward, he claimed it was a wolf that wet on him, but I never was altogether convinced."

Willie and Silas giggled while Julia scolded Jack for his coarseness. Jack apologized in that cheerful way of his, and said on a serious note, "About tonight, Julia. Tee's excitable, and not the best shot in the world. If I was you, I'd sleep in the cabin out of harm's way."

Julia agreed.

Right after supper, Jack stretched out to catch a few winks before nightfall.

Ellen returned to the creek with the boys and lashed the logs together. Silas's hands were the strongest, so he tied the knots. But when they put the raft in the water, the knots stretched and the raft broke apart.

"Shucks," said Willie. "Sun's setting. We're out of daylight."

"That's all right. We'll fix it tomorrow," said Silas. He pushed the logs to shore. Ellen and Willie helped pull them up the bank.

On the way back to the house, they talked over the problem.

"Maybe we should notch the logs, like Father and Jack are doing for Julia's room," suggested Ellen.

"Too much work," said Silas.

"It'd take us days," Willie chimed agreement.

"So? What's the big hurry?" argued Ellen.

"How about we just tie the logs to cross logs?" said

Silas. "You know, one cross log on each end?"

"On top or underneath?" asked Willie.

"On top, I think. We can keep an eye on the knots that way." Silas stopped to dig at his ankle. "What do you think, Ellie?"

"My name is Ellen," said Ellen with a jerk of her head. "That's with two *l*'s and two *e*'s and an *n*. And itchin' blisters is what you get for wading through poison ivy, that's what I think."

Ellen awoke just before dawn to hear Jack falling into the bed he shared with Willie. She heard him mumble something about chores, about the wolf he and Tee had killed, and about the three that had gotten away.

Too groggy to catch it all, she rolled over and dozed until she heard Julia making breakfast. They ate quietly, so as not to disturb Jack, then Ellen helped Julia tidy up while Silas and Willie went to the barn.

Upon their return, Silas told a tale about Milkweed not giving any milk. Julia didn't know enough about cows to question his story, and Jack was still asleep. So it seemed that Silas was in the clear in regard to Milkweed's onion grazing.

Ellen fetched the ax while Silas and Willie walked Milkweed to pasture. Willie, in his haste to accompany Silas, overlooked Matilda. She followed Ellen to the creek but showed no inclination to wander off and be lunch for wolves. Instead, she swam and hunted grubs and got in the way as they worked, tying the logs together and knotting them to the cross logs Silas had cut.

"Ready? On the count of three, push!" said Silas when the raft was finished. "One, two, three!"

Together, they shoved the raft down the low bank into the creek and clambered aboard. Water poured through the cracks between the logs and washed over Ellen's bare toes. But the logs held together.

"It works! We're floating!" cried Willie.

"Look at Matilda! She's coming, too!" Ellen pointed as the fat goose launched herself into the water after them. She laughed. "She thinks she's one of us!"

Matilda beat the air with her wings, spraying them all as she hopped from the creek to the raft. She landed in the midst of them, stepped over Father's ax handle, and arched her neck toward Ellen's toes.

"Not *my* toes, you don't!" With a giggle, Ellen sat down and tucked her feet under her.

Matilda went after Silas's toes instead. He yelped and leaned on the pole in a little dance that turned the raft in a circle. Disdaining Willie's and Ellen's rowdy laughter, Matilda honked and fluttered back into the water.

"Silas made her dizzy with his circling," said Ellen. She came to her feet and reached for the pole. "Let me try!"

Pushing the raft along with the pole wasn't as easy as it looked. At first, she bumped from bank to bank, but soon learned from her bumbling attempts and held to the middle of the creek. The current, combined with her poling, carried them lazily along.

"Can't you go any faster?" asked Willie.

"Here, you do it," said Ellen.

She gave Willie the pole, sat down on the edge of the raft, and dangled her legs in the water. The ripples lapped against the raft, sloshing like the butter churn. Ellen stretched out on her back on the bumpy logs. They passed beneath webs of green branches with the birds twittering overhead and Matilda swimming ahead of them.

"Let's pretend we're taking a trip," said Willie. "Matilda can be our scout."

"Where do you want to go?" asked Silas.

"To Louisa's house," said Ellen, daydreaming.

"Snake!" Willie's warning pierced the peaceful morning air.

Ellen recoiled at the sight of the snake sunning on a branch almost directly overhead. Silas leaped to his feet and uncoiled the whip at his belt. There was no time to warn that he was too close. That he didn't have enough room to aim and execute. He wouldn't hear anyway. He never did when he got that snake-killing madness in his eyes.

Chapter Seven

Silas threw his weight to one corner of the raft as he scrambled to unfurl his whip. Torn leaves came down like rain, and the snake with them. It grazed Ellen's left shoulder just as the raft tipped and spilled them into the creek. She went under screaming and came up choking and thrashing toward shore. Her feet skimmed the sandy creek bottom in her dive for land. She shrieked as her foot glided over something smooth and slick.

It was a rock. But it might as well have been the snake, the fright it gave her. Ellen grabbed a tree root and pulled herself up the bank, coughing and spitting out water. Willie dragged up the bank after her. Silas was still in the water, trying to untangle his whip from an overhead branch.

"Think we should . . . ," Willie began.

"I think we should throw a snake on him, that's what I think!" said Ellen, shaking from head to toe.

"I didn't mean to tip us," said Silas, looking sheepish. "Pull the raft to shore while I get my whip free. Make sure the knots are holding, and we'll try it again."

"Try it again? That snake hit me!" Ellen shuddered, skin crawling.

"It was just an old water snake," said Willie, shaking himself off.

"Yeah, a water snake," echoed Silas, like he'd known all along. "Anyway, it was an accident."

"*You're* the accident," Ellen yelled, hands on her hips. "You want to kill every snake in the country? Go ahead! But leave me out of it! I'm going home. Willie, are you coming?"

Willie dug his toe in the mud and ducked his head.

So stay with Silas. See if I care! Ellen tramped home, water streaming from her hair.

Jack was out by the pole barn, skinning the wolf he had killed. It wasn't a pleasant sight. But it was nowhere near so alarming as that snake! Ellen rubbed her shoulder, trying to rid herself of the notion the snake had left an imprint.

"Hey!" called Jack. "Father's home and he's looking for his ax."

"His ax? Oh, no!" Ellen clapped her hands over her face.

"You've had it?" asked Jack. "Ellie! Use your head! You know better'n to take Father's tools!"

"But the logs were too long for our raft! We had to . . ."

Father strode out of the barn and looked at her dripping hair and wet dress. "What's that boy done now?" he asked.

It had become a standard question since Silas's arrival. Ellen was tempted to make the most of it, and lay the lost ax on Silas. But Father hated half truths even worse than looking for lost tools.

"I fell in the creek," she said finally.

"Fell in?"

"The raft tipped."

"What raft?"

"We made a raft."

"Are the boys still there?"

Ellen nodded.

"Do they have my ax?"

She swallowed hard.

"Do they?"

"Yessir. That is, they do . . . they did . . . but they . . . we . . . ," stammered Ellen. She tugged at her soppy dress, her voice shrinking. "It was on the raft when we tipped."

"The ax fell in the creek?" His voice stung her ears like flung cinders. "Did you get it out?"

Silence was all the answer he needed.

"What're you doing here, then? Get on down there and don't come back until you've got it!"

Ellen raced back through the woods. The boys had rafted downstream a ways. None of them remembered exactly where it was that they had spilled into the creek. Snakes squiggled in Ellen's imagination, bigger than life. But the only thing scarier than getting into the water was telling Father she couldn't find his ax. She got in, every nerve atingle.

"Well? Come on, what're you waiting for?" she said to Silas.

"Aren't you coming, Willie?" asked Silas, looking jumpy himself.

"No, he's not!" countered Ellen. "You're not, Willie. It's over your head in places and you don't swim that good. Look for my footprints on the bank, and then we'll know where we tipped over."

Willie started upstream, his head down as he searched the ground. Silas waded into the water and minced along beside Ellen, searching the sandy creek bottom.

Matilda swam with them. Ellen's pulse leaped at every ripple, splash, and trickle. She had swum, played, washed wool with Mama, and bathed in the creek without giving snakes more than a passing thought. But that was before clumsy Silas and his stupid whip!

After a while, Jack came to see what was taking them so long. When he heard the full story, he said, "Stripping trees again, were you, Silas? Maybe if you were to look up instead of down, you could find shredded leaves and you'd know where you tipped over."

Jack's suggestion made sense, even to Silas.

"I've got something!" cried Silas, only moments after they found the place where they had capsized. He prodded once more with his foot, then bobbed under and came up with the ax. "I found it!"

"Lucky for *you*," said Ellen. She reached for the ax. "Give it to me, before you lose it again."

"Help me get Matilda, would you, Silas?" called Willie, and waited for him to catch up.

Ellen's mouth flattened at the warm spark in Silas's eye as he started after Willie. But, unwilling to face Father's wrath alone, she waited for the boys, and they all went home together.

Father was sitting on a log in the yard, eating lunch.

His adze was on the ground beside a pile of skinned-off bark and wood chips. Julia stood unnoticed in the open door a few yards behind him.

"Since when is it all right to let Jack carry the whole load while you're off having a good time?" Father asked Willie. His question fell into a pool of silence. "*Since when?*"

Willie jumped. "It isn't, sir."

"And you!" Father turned to Ellen. "Floating down the creek when you ought to be lending Julia a hand. What got into you?"

"Nothing, sir," she said.

"Nothing. That's what you have without an ax," said Father. "Without it, you can't build a house or warm yourself or cook your food. Don't touch it again. Or any other tool on the place, unless you've been told to. Is that clear?"

"Yes, sir."

"Good. Go pull weeds in the west field. And don't come in until I send for you." Father flicked his hand in dismissal and reached for his tankard of milk on the log beside him. He took one sip, growled in disgust, and flung milk over the peeled logs strewn about the yard. "That cow has been in the onions again!"

Ellen walked a little faster. So did Willie, but she saw his back stiffen.

"Who's been taking her to pasture?" Father demanded.

"Me."

Dry mouthed, Ellen looked around to see Silas swing

back and face Father. Willie pivoted, too, and edged closer to Silas.

"Weren't you watching her?" Father's eyes sparked.

"Sort of."

"He didn't know about the onions," Willie inserted in a whisper.

"Anyway, we didn't think there was any milk today," added Silas.

"Come on, Si," Jack broke in. "Of course there was milk."

"There wasn't this morning, Jack. Milkweed was dry. Honest," said Willie.

"No, she wasn't. I milked her myself before I came to bed," said Jack.

"Oh!" whispered Willie.

"So that's it," said Silas at the same moment.

The boys looked at each other, then ducked their heads.

Father's smoldering gaze skipped from Silas to Willie and back again. "Silas, you're a walking calamity. Is there anything on the place you haven't tripped over, dropped, spilled, or spoiled while I was gone?"

Silas wrinkled his mouth to one side, then stooped and scratched his poison-ivy blisters.

Father dragged a hand over his face and shifted his weight. "I don't know what to do about you, I declare I don't."

"I should probably go to the field and pull some weeds," said Silas, as solemn as the circuit preacher.

"You think so, do you?" said Father. He turned and

looked over his shoulder and, for the first time, saw Julia standing in the cabin door with her arms crossed. His mouth tightened. He jerked his head in her direction. "See what your mother can find for you to do. Go on. Get."

Ellen and Willie started for the field. Even when they were out of Father's sight, it didn't feel safe to slow down.

Willie angled her a sidelong glance. "You mad?"

"At Silas!" she said with feeling.

"You think he got off too easy?"

"You don't see him coming with us to pull weeds, do you?"

"He'd of come, though, if Father'd of let him."

"I'm hot and I'm hungry and wet and I don't feel a bit sorry for Silas, if that's what you're getting at!"

"I wasn't," he said.

Ellen shuddered. "I feel like I got snakes crawling on me."

"I don't see any," said Willie.

"I know that!"

Seeing Willie drop his gaze, Ellen reined in her temper. After all, it wasn't his fault. "Father would have lit into Silas a whole lot worse, if it wasn't for Julia," she admitted grudgingly. "She won't let Father punish him."

"She said that?"

"Just as good as."

Willie's eyes got wide. "When?"

"The first day they came."

Willie shooed a fly away and said on a hopeful note,

"Maybe if she gets to liking us, she'll tell him not to punish us, either."

"Maybe," said Ellen. "If she stays."

"She'll stay," said Willie.

Ellen wasn't so sure. She'd seen Julia's face when Father had scolded Silas for his clumsiness. Julia hadn't liked it. She hadn't liked it *at all*.

Chapter Eight

Ellen looked beyond the thriving corn to see Silas skirting the field, his whip at his side. It was late afternoon. She was half starved and dripping with sweat. The flies were biting and her feet were sore from padding barefoot over the cloddy field.

"Mother says for you to come in," Silas called from the shade of the trees that lined the field.

Ellen shot Willie a glance. Sharing her caution, he called back, "What about Father?"

"He's got company," said Silas.

"Company?" Ellen couldn't see the cabin from the field.

Silas nodded. "It's your Uncle Washington."

"Did he bring the calves?" asked Willie.

"Yes, and something extra. Not something, some-one."

"Who?" demanded Ellen.

"Louisa." He grinned. "Just teasing."

The squeal of joy died in Ellen's throat. "That's not funny!" she said, and flung a weed at him.

Silas ducked behind some nearby brush Father had cleared. "I was teasing when I said I was teasing," he called. "She's right here. Come see! Come on, don't be a sorehead."

Ellen picked up a dirt clod and hurled it toward the brush pile. At the same moment, Louisa popped up from behind the brush. The clod hit a dead limb and broke apart, showering her in a spray of dirt.

"Yipes!" yelped Louisa. Dressed in a faded red dress and flushed with laughter, she looked like a dancing flame as she giggled and brushed and shook herself off.

"See? I told you," said Silas. His mouth stretched into a big fat grin.

Shock fading, Ellen rushed over the field, crying, "How did you *get* here?"

"On a horse, of course." Louisa giggled at her rhyme. "I lost my sunbonnet in a creek we were crossing, and I'm so sore from riding, I walk funny now. See how funny I walk?" She slowed to baby steps and wobbled right into Ellen.

They hugged so tight that Louisa burped, which made her giggle. "Oops. Excuse me!"

Ellen laughed, scorched feet, growling belly, and sore limbs forgotten. "How long can you stay?"

"Just for tomorrow."

"But you just got here!"

"I know, but Mama will worry if we're gone too long."

"Why didn't she come?"

"Daddy tried to get her to, but she said Areanna was too little for the trip, so they just stayed home," Louisa explained. "Look what I brought you. Arrowheads!"

Louisa reached inside her dress and pulled out a burlap bag. "See? There's bunches. Daddy saves 'em for me when he finds them in the field."

"We find 'em, too," said Willie.

Seeing Louisa's face fall, Ellen added in a rush, "But these are lots prettier'n ours. I like this red one."

"Keep it, then," said Louisa, all dimples again.

"But I don't have anything to give you," protested Ellen.

"That's all right. 'Tis more blessed to give than . . . Oops!" Louisa winced as Silas bumped heads with her, trying to see the arrowheads. " . . . get your head cracked," she finished.

"Silas! Watch out!" said Ellen.

Silas backed out of the way.

Willie slapped his hand against his leg the way Silas was doing with his coiled whip. "Know what, Louisa? We've got a raft. We made it ourselves, didn't we, Silas?"

"I helped," said Ellen. "I know! That'll be our gift to you! A ride on our raft!"

Louisa's blue eyes sparkled. "When can we go?"

Ellen gripped her hollow stomach. "Soon as we eat supper."

"If Father will let us," Willie inserted.

Ellen's joy dimmed at the realization Father's sparks and flames might not be over yet. As they started home, she told Louisa about losing the ax in the water. Willie walked beside them, breaking in now and then while Silas walked ahead, snipping at weeds with the tip of his whip.

When Ellen fell silent, Louisa told about her long ride.

"From Rock Creek to Timber Creek, all in a day!" she wound her account of the trip to a close.

"We've done it, too, haven't we, Ellie?" said Willie.

Ellen nodded. Though they hadn't since Mama died. Would Father ever take them again?

"There's Uncle Wash!" Willie dashed toward the clearing where the calves Uncle Wash had brought along were grazing alongside his trail-worn mare, Ginger. Ellen and Louisa fell behind, arms linked, talking and laughing. They reached the clearing just as Uncle Wash was exclaiming over the muscles Willie displayed.

He turned to Ellen with a smile. "Is this our Ellie? Why, look how you've grown! You're gettin' to be the picture of your mother. Ladylike, too, instead of trying to talk over everybody else the way someone I could mention," he said with a glance at chattering Louisa.

"Ladylike?" said Jack. "That's just Ellie's company manners, isn't it, Ellie?"

Silas hooted.

Ellen ignored him and glowered at Jack. He was a fine one to talk, telling stories at the table about wolves wetting on people.

"Drive the calves into the pasture, Willie," said Father. "Jack, take care of Wash's horse while I start evening chores."

"Reckon I'll come along with you," said Uncle Washington.

The men ambled toward the barn, but Silas stayed in the yard with Ellen and Louisa. They made a game of walking the stacks of peeled logs until Julia called everyone to supper.

It was a lively meal. Louisa chattered about her mother and Areanna, about school and the neighbors, and going to the store at New Salem and looking at blue willow dishes. Uncle Wash shushed her every now and then, telling her to calm down.

Ellen hoped Louisa never calmed down. She loved her cousin's flashing dimples and run-together freckles and the way she made her eyes go wide when she got to the really good parts of a story.

"Any fresh news on Black Hawk?" asked Uncle Wash as he helped himself to more green beans and new potatoes fresh from the garden.

"Just came back from the fort at Rock Island. They say he's staying west of the river," said Father.

"Glad to hear it," said Uncle Wash. "Maybe he's starting to feel his age."

"He's old for a warrior," said Jack. "But he's still a warrior."

"You think he'll be back?" asked Julia.

"I think he will, if he can get some other bands to join up with the Sac and Fox," Jack replied.

"What are they anticipating at the fort, Mr. Tandy?" asked Julia.

"They know not to second-guess Indians. Or if they don't, they should," said Father.

He changed the subject then. Soon, he and Jack and Uncle Wash ambled outdoors. The boys followed. But Ellen knew better than to slip away without helping Julia clean up.

Louisa admired Julia's pretty dishes. "They're like the inside of a clamshell."

"Milky white pearl," agreed Ellen, knowing just what she meant.

"'Course you don't have to be so careful with wooden ones," Louisa reasoned. "Except for splinters."

It had been a while since Ellen had eaten out of wooden dishes. Father had replaced Mama's with kiln-fired clay dishes some time ago. Mama had never replaced her wooden bread trough, though.

Ellen turned the bread trough in her hands. She ran her fingers over the hatchet marks Father had made as he chipped away at the chunk of walnut. It made her think of the smoky wood smell as he burned out the inside and of Mama whistling as she scraped away the charred parts. She missed Mama's whistling. Julia never whistled. She didn't sing, either. She moved through her everyday chores, drawing no more attention than the sun trekking across the sky on an overcast day.

"I'm going to help Mama card wool this winter so she can buy those dishes," said Louisa. "And I won't stop until we've got enough, not even if my fingers crack and bleed and fall off."

"You're a good daughter," said Julia. She wiped the table with a damp dish towel and said, "You girls are free to go now."

"Thanks for the good supper," said Louisa, flinging her arms around Julia.

Ellen picked up the water bucket and led Louisa outside.

"Can we go down to the creek and play on . . ."

"Shh!" warned Ellen, cutting Louisa short. "Whatever you do, don't mention the raft in front of Father. And don't even *look* at his ax! It'll just remind him."

Louisa clamped her hand over her mouth. They skirted the piles of logs where Father and the boys were working.

The boys dropped the sticks they were picking up and came running.

"Where're you boys off to in such a hurry?" Father called after them.

"We're going with Ellen," said Willie.

"Where are you headed, Ellen?" asked Father.

"To the spring," said Ellen, swinging the bucket. "Then for a walk," she added, hoping he wouldn't guess it was to the creek.

"Give the bucket to Silas; he can fill it for Julia," said Father. "Willie, you come on back here and finish picking up sticks. Louisa, can you swim?"

"No, sir."

"You girls stay off the raft then, until you've got a good swimmer along."

Ellen was a good swimmer. But she didn't make any claims Father might mistake for back talk. Reining in her disappointment, she said, "Can we go to the bluff?"

Father nodded and went back to notching logs.

"It's all right, I don't care what we do, so long as

we're together," said Louisa. She reached for Ellen's hand and burst out singing as they skipped along.

They took the long way to the bluff, an easy and gradual climb. Once there, Ellen pointed out the skinny tree where Willie had taken refuge from the snake. She told Louisa about Silas snagging his whip in a bush and tumbling downhill like a lopsided rock.

Louisa laughed. "Silas is funny. I like him, don't you?"

"He's all right," said Ellen, not wanting to be gloomy next to Louisa's sparkle.

"He's pretty, too. Or maybe I should say handsome," Louisa corrected herself with a giggle. "Julia, now, *she's* pretty."

Ellen took the gift arrowhead from her pocket. The muted red color and the scalloped edges made her think of one of Julia's quilts. She described it for Louisa.

"I want to see! Let's go have a look," said Louisa.

"We better not," said Ellen uneasily. "It's in the wagon and anyway, it's hers."

"The quilt or the wagon?"

"Both," said Ellen.

"But what's hers is Uncle Gil's, too, isn't it? And that makes it partly yours," reasoned Louisa.

If your family was whole, maybe. Ellen could see that hers was not.

Chapter Nine

Upon returning to the cabin, Ellen heard Uncle Wash offer to stay an extra day if Father needed help putting up Julia's room. Father accepted.

"Yippee!" cried Louisa, and flung her arms around Ellen.

Ellen laughed and hugged her back. They clasped hands and giggled and danced in a circle as Julia thanked Uncle Wash.

"Wash, why don't you take Ellen's bed tonight?" said Julia. "Silas, you sleep inside, too. Ellen and Louisa can sleep in the wagon with me."

Just before sunset, Julia sent Ellen and Louisa to the creek to bathe. They made a detour along the way so Louisa could see the raft. But they didn't linger long. Still jumpy over snakes, Ellen wanted to bathe before it got dark.

By the time they got back from the creek, the sun was gone from the sky. Julia had already retired to the wagon. Her lantern glowed softly from the other side of the canvas top. Ellen could see her moving around inside. Her steps slowed. The wagon gave her the same "company manners" feeling she used to get when she and Mama went to visit Mrs. Kelly. She held back.

But not Louisa. She climbed right in. Bedding and a

trunk at the far end of the wagon took up most of the floor space. Julia was sitting on the trunk, brushing her hair. The lantern made a pool of light on a washbasin, a cake of rose-scented lye soap, and a few articles of clothing.

"Drop the flap, girls. You're letting in bugs," said Julia as Ellen climbed in after Louisa.

Ellen dropped the canvas flap, closing out the night sky.

"Is this the quilt, Ellie?" asked Louisa.

Ellen flushed and explained, "I told her it was the color of my arrowhead. See?" she said, showing it to Julia.

"That's lovely," said Julia, running her fingers along the edges.

The quilt was lovely, too. It covered linens and a feather tick.

"It's beautiful!" cried Louisa, stretching out on the quilt. "Red's my favorite color."

The quilt was pieced of many red and white squares. Half-moon slices had been cut from the side of each square and replaced with slices of alternate colors, marrying reds and whites in neatly stitched seams.

"It was my wedding quilt," said Julia. "I nearly bought blue, but my sisters thought blue was too quiet. They helped me make it. The pattern is called Robbing Peter to Pay Paul," she added as Louisa dumped her sack of arrowheads on the quilt.

Ellen thought about the name as she and Louisa played with the arrowheads, and again when Julia put out the lamp and stretched out beside them. It was a sneaky name. Sneaky, like a cheat wearing an innocent smile.

"Mama's teaching me to quilt," said Louisa, twitching around, trying to get comfortable. "You have to make thirteen quilts by the time you're thirteen, or you won't ever get married."

"Why not?" asked Ellen, fighting sleep.

"I don't know. That's just what Mama said her mama told her. I guess if you can't make thirteen quilts, you're trifling and who wants a trifling wife?"

"How would he know you didn't make thirteen if you didn't tell him?"

"I don't know, I'll ask Mama." Louisa said, "Aunt Julia, did you make thirteen quilts by the time you were thirteen?"

"Hush, girls, and go to sleep," said Julia.

"But did you?" Louisa persisted.

Ellen meant to stay awake for the answer. But her eyes were just too heavy.

The following day was full, with Julia's room going together log by log. But it was nowhere nearly long enough for Ellen. Or Louisa. Over supper, she tried to coax her father into staying another day.

"Uncle Gil needs help putting a roof on Aunt Julia's room. Don't you, Uncle Gil?" Louisa turned pleading eyes from her father to Ellen's and back again.

"I never turn away good help," said Father. "You're welcome to stay as long as you like."

"Thanks, Gil. But we'd best head home. I don't want to worry Clarissa," said Uncle Wash.

"But it will be forever and ever before I see Ellen again!" Tears rolled down Louisa's cheeks and splashed onto her plate.

Jack was watching Ellen, his mouth all set to tease. Noticing, she blinked hard and kept her eyes dry.

"I hope you'll come again and bring Louisa," Julia said to Uncle Washington.

"Thanks, Julia. But it's a long ride, and I don't know when I'll have cause to come this way again."

"I understand that Ellen and the boys sometimes used to go south with you," Julia spoke up.

"Leah liked to get together with Clarissa from time to time," said Father.

"I'd like that myself," said Julia.

"It's a long ride, and a hard one," said Father shortly.

Ellen's hopes rose and fell all in a heartbeat. She traded a letdown look with Louisa and braced herself for another long separation.

When dinner was over, Julia rose from the table and untied her apron. "I'd like to see that raft I've been hearing so much about. Who wants to come with me?"

Father opened his mouth as if to object, then closed it again.

Ellen, Louisa, Silas, and Willie jumped up so fast, they nearly knocked the table over. Jack came, too. There wasn't room on the raft for all of them.

"Girls first," said Jack. He freed the grapevine loop the boys had used to tie the raft to a stump, then grabbed the rafting pole and beckoned to Louisa and Ellen. As Jack guided the raft downstream, the boys kept pace with them on the bank.

"You want to go next, Julia?" Jack called back.

"No, thanks. I believe I'll take off my shoes, soak my feet, and watch the fish swim by."

Realizing Julia had no real interest in the raft, Ellen blurted, "Jack can make you a fishin' pole. Can't you, Jack?"

Jack laughed. "Ellie's turned into Father, taking rest and making it into work."

The following morning, Ellen couldn't hold back her tears as Louisa rode away.

"Ellie's face has sprung a leak," teased Jack.

"Go milk the cow, Jack Tandy, and leave your sister alone."

Jack's ears turned red at Julia's tone. "I thought the boys were milking."

Father indicated the barn with a jerk of his thumb. "You heard her. Go on."

"What about that roof?"

"It'll still be waiting when you get back," said Father. He picked up the ax and started splitting shakes for Julia's roof.

"Come on, Ellen," said Julia as Jack strode toward the barn. "Let's find some of those wild onions Milkweed is so partial to."

Julia was quiet as they crossed the yard and took the beaten path between fenced pasture and open prairie.

Ellen showed her where the onions were. She pulled a few, shook the dirt off the roots, and put them in her apron pocket.

"I suppose you're missing Louisa," she said as they started back.

Ellen nodded. "She's fun. Pretty, too. I like her red hair."

"You're fun, too. And you're pretty and your hair is a lovely warm color."

Ellen wrinkled her nose. "It's ordinary brown."

"I like ordinary brown," said Julia. "It's comfortable and it goes with everything."

Ellen tucked her chin and kept her eyes on her broad, dusty, sun-browned feet, wishing she could trade places with Louisa.

"You're comfortable company," said Julia. "And for making me comfortable, I'm going to see to it that you and Louisa get together again next spring. If not sooner."

Ellen wanted to hug Julia as Louisa had done. It was more than shyness holding her back. It was thoughts of Mama. Hugging Julia would be robbery. Robbing Mama to Pay Julia. She couldn't do that. Not even for a trip to Rock Creek.

Chapter Ten

If not sooner, Julia had said. But as the summer faded, so did Ellen's hopes for *sooner*. In early October, after a killing frost, Father hired Mr. Kelly to help him and Jack drive cattle north to Fort Armstrong.

A few days later, while the boys were milking and doing chores, Ellen caught Julia in the open door, gazing into the distance. Mama used to do that when Father was away.

"It hasn't been a week yet," said Ellen.

"I was thinking about Mrs. Kelly's invitation to visit," said Julia. "I would imagine she's lonely with her husband away."

"Are you?" asked Ellen before she could stop herself.

"When I have you and Willie and Silas right here with me? No, Ellen. I don't get lonely," said Julia. She untied her apron and gave it a shake. "Would you like to come with me?"

"To Mrs. Kelly's? No, thanks," said Ellen. Pretending to misunderstand Julia's surprised glance, she added, "You can't miss the Kellys' place. All you have to do is follow the creek three miles north."

"She asked me to bring my teapot," Julia reminded her. "Are you sure you don't want to come along?"

Ellen shook her head. "I promised Willie I'd help him with his tree fort today."

Julia nodded and said no more about it. But pensive lines framed her mouth as she took the teapot off the shelf and reached for a dish towel and a muslin bag.

Ellen didn't know why it was hard to watch the gentleness of her graceful hands any more than she understood how Julia slipped into guarded places. *For a moment, it had been all right with her if Julia missed Father.* The realization burned like a cinder, for it was a robbing thought, and unfair to Mama.

Ellen picked up a stick from the kindling box and broke it into tiny pieces. It was becoming harder to remember Mama's face. Her cheery whistle. The glint of firelight in her hair when she brushed it out at night. She would think about those things while Julia was away.

Ellen held the muslin bag while Julia climbed up behind Silas on one of the horses that had pulled their wagon into Illinois the previous spring. The saddle Silas straddled was hers, too. It had belonged to her first husband, Silas's father.

Julia hadn't asked Silas to accompany her. But there he sat, his whip coiled at his side. His shoulders were back, his chin up. He looked like a regular soldier, proud to be doing his duty. Ellen could hardly keep from cheering at the prospect of a day without him.

"Here you go," she said, and gave Silas the sack holding the teapot. He looped the drawstring over the saddle horn.

"You haven't had a change of heart?" asked Julia as she smoothed her skirts. "What about you, Willie? You're welcome to come along."

"Maybe another time," said Willie, who had more interest in forts than tea parties.

"It's all right to go without us," said Ellen, seeing through Julia's efforts to coax them into going. "Father leaves us days at a time."

"I know. I'm not worried," said Julia. "Don't add any wood to the fire while I'm gone, all right? And stay off the raft. In fact, I'd feel a lot better if you'd stay away from the creek altogether until I get back."

"She's not a bit worried, it's plain to see," said Ellen as they rode away.

"Why would she worry?" asked Willie, scratching his chin. "She's got Silas to protect her."

"But who's going to protect her from Silas?" Ellen giggled. "If he sees a snake, she better hang on tight!"

Willie had chosen a tree at the top of the bluff for his fort. It overlooked the open prairie to the south. They used grapevines to tie sturdy limbs across a fan of branches ten feet off the ground. The limbs creaked and groaned beneath their weight. They pretended they were soldiers on watch for Black Hawk and his men.

The sun stayed hidden all morning. Early in the afternoon, Ellen noticed the clouds had thickened to the south. Something about them wasn't right. They hovered just over the ground. The longer Ellen gazed, the less cloudlike they looked. There was a muted red glow in their hazy depths. She rubbed her itching nose and frowned. All at once, her pulse jumped.

"Willie! Does that look like fire to you?"

"Fire?" Willie dropped his stick gun and swung out of the tree after her.

"Don't you smell it? It's a scorchy smell."

"Maybe someone's burning off ground," said Willie.

Burning off prairie grass was a common practice. It encouraged lush new growth for grazing stock. But it looked like a lot of smoke to Ellen. She dampened one finger and held it to the air. "Wind's pert out of the southwest."

Willie scanned the prairie. "Do you think it's got away from them?"

"Wouldn't be the first time."

Willie shivered and pressed closer. "What do we do if it burns to the cabin?"

"Look after ourselves, that's what we do," said Ellen, knowing they couldn't fight a fire alone. "The creek's the best place to be if it's headed this way."

"Julia said stay out of the creek."

"She wasn't thinking about fires." Ellen watched the dark billows on the horizon. "Is it just me, or is it getting closer?"

"Looks closer," said Willie. He dropped his stick gun and turned for home. "I've got to find Matilda."

"We better turn Milkweed out, too," said Ellen, keeping a grip on rising alarm. "And the sheep."

"What about the hogs?"

"Turn 'em loose," said Ellen. The hogs often roamed

free in the woods, grazing on nuts and roots and weeds.

By the time Ellen and Willie had emptied the pole barn, the sheep pen, and freed the hogs, smoke was drifting over the clearing like whispy fog. They chased the livestock into the woods.

"Once you get to the creek, head north toward Kellys'!" Ellen hollered to Willie, then turned back toward the cabin.

"Where are you going?" Willie cried, starting to follow her.

"I'm getting us each a blanket. We'll need it if the fire moves over us."

"But what if I can't find you?"

"I'll find *you*," said Ellen. "Go on, Willie! Get the livestock started up creek. Hurry! I'll catch up!"

Ellen pounded out of the woods and across the clearing, past Julia's new room and around to the front door. She grabbed two quilts off the beds and dashed outside.

She couldn't see flames or feel heat. But the smoke followed her into the timber. It burned her throat and eyes as she fought undergrowth that snagged her skirt and stockings. The fluttering in her chest turned to a pounding drum as she stumbled over roots and branches hidden by fresh-fallen leaves. The leaves themselves were the worst danger. If they caught fire, the whole timber floor would blaze!

A hog squealed as it streaked past. Ellen tripped and dropped her quilts. She scooped them up, raced on to the creek, and turned north through a patch of nettles.

They stung her through her stockings. But the discomfort was minor compared to the windblown smoke.

"Willie?" cried Ellen, eyes streaming. "Willie! Where are you? Can you hear me?"

"Right here."

Ellen found him hunkered down on a rise overlooking the creek. He was struggling to hold on to Matilda. Bleating sheep milled around him. The hogs had already scattered through the woods. Nor was Milkweed anywhere to be seen.

Ellen flung Willie a quilt and looked back the way she'd come. She couldn't see flames, but the smoke was making her cough. Maybe the woods was the worst, not the best place to be.

"Put Matilda down and keep moving!" she cried, and wiped her burning eyes. "If we see flames, we'll get in the creek."

"What about the sheep?"

"Forget 'em! Hurry, Willie, hurry!"

They had gone only a short distance when Ellen heard leaves crackling. Ground fire! *Get in the water.* The silent prodding was like a physical push. She grabbed Willie's hand and pulled him down the sloping bank to the edge of the water several feet below.

It was cold and deep enough to duck under if the flames came.

"What's that?" cried Willie as the crackling grew louder. But it was not leaves burning! It was a rider, a horse rustling through the leaves.

"Somebody's coming! Help! Help!" Ellen leaped up

and down, waving the quilt overhead as the horse came barreling out of the haze.

Julia! A tangle of hair and wild eyes and billowing skirt, she clung to the saddle horn. The mare tossed her head, eyes rolling. She reared back on her powerful hind legs and pawed the air with a near-human scream. Ellen heard breaking glass. A shrill cry. Crackling brush as Julia hit the ground. The mare plunged down the bank, snorting and blowing, her hooves flinging mud.

"Catch her, Ellie! Catch her!" cried Julia, skidding down the slippery bank on her backside.

Ellen grabbed for whipping reins as the horse thrashed into the water. Incredibly, she snagged them, and at the same moment, squeezed her eyes shut and braced herself, for fear the horse would fling her into the air with one toss of her head. She didn't. The water slowed her. In an instant, Julia was in the creek with Ellen and Willie.

"Easy, there's a good girl," she crooned, slipping her hand beneath a halter strap. "Give me your skirt before she bolts again," she said to Ellen in the same low honey-smooth tone so at odds with her ashen face and knotty hair and torn and muddy skirts.

What a horse couldn't see, she didn't fear. Praying the old adage was true, Ellen slipped out of her wet skirt and helped tie it around the mare's head. "Where's Silas?"

"Shh! Calmly, calmly," murmured Julia. She moved her hands down the mare's neck, over her sweat-lathered shoulders and rounded body. "I sent him back to Kellys' place when I saw the smoke. You're all right, you're just fine," she soothed the quivering mare. "Don't startle her, whatever you do. That's it, sweetheart, nothing can hurt you. Julia's here. Nothing can hurt you now."

Ellen's bones ached in the cold creek. Willie was shivering, too. Together, they struggled toward shore.

"This way, the fire's on that side of the creek. Hurry!" urged Julia, as she led the horse up the opposite bank.

Willie turned back. But Ellen froze midstream, the feed sack on the bank a stark reminder of Julia's spill and the sound of breaking glass.

"Oh, Julia! Not your teapot," cried Ellen, scrambling to retrieve it.

"Leave it."

"But maybe Father can glue it!"

"I said leave it!"

Quick tears stung Ellen's eyes as she waded across to Julia and Willie on the opposite bank.

Julia held the horse steady with one arm and grabbed their quilts with the other. "Get on!"

Ellen found the stirrup and pulled herself aboard. Willie climbed into the saddle behind her. Julia passed up the quilts and hugged Ellen's leg. "Wrap up good and tight." She gave Willie's leg a fierce squeeze, too, then stepped ahead to lead the horse.

"Climb up," urged Ellen. "There's room."

"I'm afraid to uncover her eyes. I'll have to lead her," Julia said, passing the reins up to Ellen. "Hold them loose and don't jerk on her mouth."

"I won't," said Ellen.

Julia lengthened her stride and kept a firm grip on the halter strap as they headed north toward the Kellys' place. But Ellen had hidden enough tears to read Julia's stiff shoulders and tilted head and furtive swipes at her cheeks. She eased the quilt off her own shoulders and leaned forward. "Willie and me can share."

"No, Ellen. You keep it. It'll only trip me up."

Even Willie heard the tears in Julia's voice as she declined the only comfort Ellen had to offer. "Is she scared? Are we going to burn?" he whispered, his chin propped on her quilt-draped shoulder.

"I don't think so," murmured Ellen.

"Then why's she crying?"

"Must be the teapot," whispered Ellen.

"Is that all? Shucks, Father can get her another'n, can't he?"

"It wouldn't be the same," said Ellen. "Her mama gave it to her."

"Oh," said Willie. "I guess that's different."

Chapter Eleven

The wind shifted. The fire licked eastward over the prairie. But the fresh-fallen leaves were too green to let the ground fire get a good toehold in the timber. Unlike conifer forests, which Julia had seen light the skies in the east, the greenness of the virgin hardwoods made the timber a good line of defense against a prairie fire.

The clearing around the cabin and barn was beaten down by foot and stock traffic, thus sparing their buildings. The oats had already been gathered in. But one cornfield got a good scorching. Weathered split-rail fences burned as well. But Father dismissed Jack's speculation that a roaming band of Black Hawk's men had torched the prairie, and took his losses in stride.

Shortly after his return, Father and the boys rounded up the hogs. He and Jack and Mr. Kelly put them on the trail to Galena where they would be sold to the lead miners. If the thought of the recent fire bothered Father, it didn't show in his good-byes. Before he left, Willie asked for a teapot, wanting to give it to Julia for Christmas.

Christmas was four days past by the time Father and Jack returned. Ellen wasn't surprised that Father hadn't remembered Willie's request. But at least he hadn't forgotten Christmas altogether.

For her and for Julia, there were winter moccasins. Father had gotten them from a Kickapoo Indian in exchange for corn. The moccasins were made of fur and came almost to the knees. For the boys, Father had red-topped boots that he had bought in Galena and a mongrel dog to guard the sheep.

In turn, Julia gave them each gloves and hats from animal skins Jack had tanned. They were handsome and warm.

"It's the best hat I've ever had," exclaimed Ellen, looking at herself in Julia's hand mirror.

"One of my older sisters has a shop in Boston," said Julia. "She trained me as a milliner."

Milliner? It wasn't a familiar word. Ellen thought it must have something to do with milling. But what milling and hats had in common, she didn't know. When she asked, Julia explained that millinery was hat making.

"If you'd had shoes and been about, you'd know that," said Jack.

"I've got shoes!" said Ellen.

"Have they been through the mill?" teased Jack.

He kept it up until Ellen had to kick him. He grabbed her foot and wrestled her to the floor. Willie piled on and got the liver hugged out of him, too.

"Let me know if you need any help," Silas said to Jack, reaching down as if to tickle Ellen.

"You touch me, Silas, and you're a cooked goose," she warned.

Silas darted at her again, guffawing like honking,

flapping Matilda, butting into their play.

"You boys have got so much energy, you can start chores," said Father.

Jack stopped on his way out and looked back at Silas. "What're you waiting for? You heard Father, we've got chores."

"Who, me?" said Silas.

"Who do you think I'm talking to—Ellie Mill-hat?"

Ellen flung one of her new mittens at Jack. Silas tripped over it, he was in such a hurry to catch up with Jack and Willie. *As if chores were a treat.* He was nothing short of peculiar!

It was snowing by the time they returned. It snowed all night and showed no sign of stopping the next morning. Ellen donned her new winter garb and went out with Father and the boys and tried to get acquainted with the dog. He was big and black and furry and had fierce teeth and a deep growl, which he used when Silas cracked his whip too close to the sheep pen.

"He looks meaner than a whole gang of wolves," said Ellen.

Jack, overhearing, laughed and named the dog Wolfgang. Ellen and the boys shortened it to Wolf. But Wolf made it plain he preferred guarding sheep to any of them. He was Father's kind of dog, all work and no play.

The wind howled all night. It frosted the trees in fresh-fallen snow and closed the paths they had cleared to the barn and woodpile. Ellen trooped outside with the boys again and quarrelled with Silas no more than was average as they made snow tunnels. Then Father came along and put the boys to work. Left to entertain herself, Ellen broke a stick off a tree and wrote a letter to Louisa in the snow:

"Der Lou, Fathur and Jack ar digin in the snow for
corn shocks to fed the stock. Fathur brawt us a
dawg. He is no fun."

It was only one of many digs, for it continued to snow every few days until it was two feet deep in the level places. It was twice that where it had drifted. A hard crust formed, only to be covered by fresh snows. Ellen made marks to keep count of the snowfalls right next to the log where Silas kept track of the dozens of snakes he had killed over the past season.

Julia used the snowy days for teaching. She sat at her spinning wheel, listening while Ellen and the boys took turns reading from the Bible. Silas read with the same easy flow that Julia spun flax and wool on Mama's spinning wheel. But Ellen fought the words, stumbling over them like roots in a smoky forest. Poor Willie was even worse. Julia gave them the same passages over and over until the words were old friends. Sometimes Ellen scratched the parts she could remember in the snow.

As the days passed, their supply of corn flour dwindled. It was used for the coarse bread that was the mainstay of every meal. By mid-January, they were grinding their own corn. Ellen wrote in the snow:

"Der Lou, Powndin corn evre day as Fathur can't get
to the mill. Julia sleeps in the main cabin now, as it
is too cold in her room. I sleep with her under piuls
of quilts. Her purty red wun is my favrit."

Julia came out and corrected her spelling and made her write the misspelled words ten times each in the snow. It took the fun out of it. Ellen was tired of snow.

The cattle grew thin as the snowy winter dragged on. The snow blanket was now three feet deep in level places. Father hadn't kept many hogs, but some of those he had kept froze to death. Hungry wolves preyed on the weak and dying animals, both domestic and wild. They howled close to the cabin, craving mutton. One night, Ellen awakened to Wolf's angry barking and saw Father scrambling out the door with his Kentucky long rifle in hand. Jack raced out after him.

Winds and fresh snow had filled in the path. By the time they reached the shelter where the sheep were kept, a wolf and three sheep were dead. Wolf lay bleeding in the snow. He had fought valiantly, defending the flock as best he could. It took both Jack and Father to carry him into the cabin. Julia wept as she cleaned and bound Wolf's wounds.

"Is there no end to the starving and mauling and suffering and death?" she cried.

Her tears made Father uncomfortable. He went back outside, and when the sun rose, there was no sign of the wolf or sheep corpses. Father cleaned the wool in the creek. But Julia refused to cook meat torn by animals. So Father packed the mutton on a sled. It took him all day to reach the Kellys' cabin with the meat.

Wolf spent his day on the hearth, hovering between life and death. By the next day, he was licking his wounds. On the third day, Ellen caught him watching with pain-dulled eyes as she and the boys pounded corn. Carding wool was quieter work. Wolf slept through it. On the fifth day, he whined as Ellen stretched out beside him to practice her reading.

A few evenings later, Wolf moved across the cabin and sat down by the door.

"It's time he went back to the fold, boys," said Father.

"You will not turn that dog out!" Julia replied. "He isn't well yet."

"Look at him, Julia. He wants to be out," said Father.

Julia stooped and stroked Wolf's ears and got her face licked as she questioned him as to his preference. Reluctantly, she let him out. But when Wolf tried to drag himself through the deep snow to the sheep pen, his faithfulness made her weep all over again.

Nothing would do but that Father and Jack had to carry him back to the cabin. A few more days passed, and Wolf grew so restless that Julia quit protesting and let him return to the sheep. But when the temperatures dipped and the winds blew, and it wasn't fit for man nor beast, she would make Father bring him indoors.

"You're ruining a perfectly good sheep dog," Father would grumble as Wolf joined them around the fireplace.

"Tell a wolf hunt story," Willie would say. "Wolf likes hearing about wolf hunts."

And indeed, Wolf was as attentive as anyone as Jack and Father told stories of neighborhood wolf hunts and trail drives and Indians and bee hunts.

"One time Tee went on a honey hunt with me and a few other fellas," Jack began one night after supper as they sat roasting on one side and shivering on the other. "Tee never was one for being overcautious. He got ahead of the rest of us boys. I don't know if he didn't smoke 'em good or what, but as we came over the hill, those bees commenced to pour out of that tree, humming mad. Tee shot for home with a yellow tail of bees swaying along after him. He was inches from safety when his mama slammed the door in his face and pulled the latchstring in. Said she'd sent him for honey, not a houseful of bees."

"What'd Tee do?" asked Willie when the laughter faded.

"Why, he lit for the creek, yelping."

"Where'd he get stung?" asked Silas.

"Everywhere," said Jack.

Wolf barked at their laughter. Jack grinned and caught him in a headlock and wrestled him to the floor.

"Be careful, Jack!" cried Julia. "You'll hurt him."

Even Father laughed at that.

As February dragged on, Father fixed things that had been broken ever since Mama died. He made a rolling pin to replace the one Julia had cracked, breaking the door loose when it iced shut. He even tried his hand at spinning, and encouraged the boys to do so, too. Jack made a tangle of it. But Silas, to everyone's surprise, got so good at it that, if you closed your eyes, you couldn't tell by the rhythm who it was spinning.

By the end of February, there were nineteen marks

on Ellen's snow-counting log. But marks couldn't come close to telling the story of the hardships suffered that winter. Or the troubles that followed as the snows melted off in April. The creek was so far out of its banks, the water reached the edge of the yard. The flies were awful, and the sickness was, too. When the water finally receded, it was mud, making travel impossible. Ellen knew without asking that a trip to Louisa's was out of the question.

Father was waiting for the ground to dry for spring planting when rumors reached them concerning Black Hawk. It was said he had returned to the Rock Island vicinity with a large band of braves and was ordering settlers to leave. Though the trouble was a good distance north of them, the rumors of attacks fanned fear along the frontier. Governor Reynolds called for mounted volunteers. Jack wanted to go, but Father wouldn't let him.

"I'll need you for spring planting, Jack. And soon as that's done, we have to take some cattle up to Fort Armstrong. That's where our duty lies."

"We get paid for that," said Jack.

"Soldiers draw wages, too."

"It's not the same," said Jack.

"It takes more courage to fight than to see that those who do have got something to eat. Is that what you're saying?" challenged Father.

The trip with promised cattle would take them through the very region where Black Hawk and his band were spreading such fear. It would be a hard, dangerous drive. Nor would they have an army of comrades accompanying them. Just Father and Jack and possibly a third man, if they could find someone brave enough to go. Jack thought over Father's words, and said no more about joining the volunteer militia.

When the time came for them to take cattle to Fort Armstrong, Ellen felt like bawling right along with the milling cattle. She didn't say it out loud, but she was afraid she'd never see Father or Jack again, that they would be captured or even killed by Indians.

That night, after supper, Julia listened to their reading. Ellen thought they were doing lessons until Julia took the Bible and hugged it to her and prayed for the safety of "our menfolk." Not Mr. Tandy and Jack. But "our menfolk."

A few days passed.

God knows where they are, Ellen reminded herself.

A few more days.

God knows where they are.

Four more days, and Jack and Father came home. They hadn't seen an Indian the entire trip, for Black Hawk had crossed to the west side of the Mississippi. Volunteer militia had followed them across and burned a deserted Indian village. Now there was fear Black Hawk would come back into Illinois and retaliate with strikes on settlers.

Julia, who feared the Indians, nonetheless argued with Jack over the destruction of their village, calling it a cowardly act. "I should hope you wouldn't take part in something so senseless," she said.

Jack made no reply.

Ellen could tell by what he wasn't saying, that he was still thinking about soldiering. Later, she followed him outside.

"Promise you won't be a soldier, Jack. Silas's dad was a soldier, and look what happened to him."

"He got bit by a snake," said Jack. "Didn't have a thing to do with Indians or soldiering."

Ellen thrust out her chin. "I don't care, I don't want you to, anyway."

"Does it look like I'm going anywhere?" he asked.

"No."

"Then quit your fretting," he said, rounding the house to a pile of rails waiting to be split. They were still replacing fencing from last autumn's fire.

"Then go," said Ellen with a sniff. "See if I care."

Jack laughed and tugged her braid. "Tee rode home with us," he said, sounding like himself again. "He just got mustered out of the militia. He told me all about tracking Black Hawk's band through the thickets. He said that one time . . ."

Ellen could hear his longing to go in every scorching word! She clamped her hands over her ears and shouted, "One time Tee, one time Tee! I'm sick of hearing about One Time Tee!"

Jack scowled and stamped his foot, growling, "Then go on inside, and quit pestering me."

He picked up his ax and went to work splitting rails. He swung like he was Silas, killing snakes.

If fighting broke out again, he would go. Ellen knew it

as well as anything. Knew too that once Jack made up his mind about a thing, no one could stop him. Not even Father.

Chapter Twelve

The circuit preacher brought news that Black Hawk had signed a treaty promising not ever to cross back to the east side of the Mississippi River. Not without permission, anyway. For a time, Ellen quit worrying about Jack going away, and called a truce with Silas long enough to help him and Willie build a raft to replace the one that had been swept away in the flood. Their crossing log had disappeared, too. But they discovered a dead tree that was just as much fun. The trunk was still embedded in the bank. The top tilted out over the water.

Sometimes, of an evening, Jack would join them at the creek. When he did, they had to take turns, as the raft wouldn't hold four. The Leaning Tree became the trade-off point for turn taking. Ellen liked to stretch out on the steeply pitched trunk, then drop down on the raft as it rocked over the lapping water beneath her.

One evening, as Ellen waited in the Leaning Tree for the boys to come along on the raft, Julia sat down on the nearby bank to fish. "Did the boys go off and leave you?" she called to Ellen.

"No. We're taking turns."

Julia smiled and baited her hook. Just as the sun was setting, Father strolled down to the creek and sat on a stump near Julia.

"Are you getting any bites?" he asked.

"Just flies and mosquitoes," said Julia. "Would you care to try?"

"I'm not much for fishing," he said.

"It takes patience."

"Not that again," said Father.

Julia's mouth curved. She gave her line a wiggle and looked up creek where the boys were coming around the bend.

"You taking a ride tonight, Julia?" Jack called as he poled toward them.

"I will if Mr. Tandy will."

Ellen wasn't sure who looked the most surprised, Father or the boys.

"What about it, Mr. Tandy?" pressed Julia, tilting her face with the challenge.

Jack poled to shore without waiting for Father's reply. Silas and Willie scrambled ashore. Julia jumped aboard. Father followed.

"Maybe I should navigate," said Jack. "We don't want you sinking the cook. We'd have to go back to eating Ellie's food."

"Hey! I heard that!" objected Ellie from her tree.

Julia smiled. "I'm a good swimmer."

"That makes one of you," said Jack.

Father reached for the pole. "Give me that, and get out of the way."

Jack grinned and leaped to shore where the boys had taken over Julia's fishing line.

Father worked the raft through the water. He was

closing the distance to Ellen's Leaning Tree at a pace that made his muscles bunch beneath his shirt and put sweat on his brow. Julia had her back to Ellen. She would pass beneath the tree first. Their voices rose and fell in the twilight. Ellen picked a leaf and watched it fall into the water.

"Can you swim, Mr. Tandy?" Julia asked as they drew near.

"I get by."

"You can't, can you? Forevermore! And you travel all over the country with those cows."

"Cattle," corrected Father. "Watch your head."

Julia didn't have to duck. Her day cap just barely grazed the tree as the raft glided beneath it. "How do you manage creeks and rivers if you can't swim?"

"He lets Gertie swim him across," said Ellen.

Startled, Father straightened too soon, bumped his head, and staggered to one side. The raft tipped. Father teetered, Julia tottered. Each reached to steady the other.

Julia laughed as the raft stabilized. "Where's Gertie when you need her?"

"Sorry, I thought you saw me," Ellen called after them.

"We were watching where we were going. Weren't we, Mr. Tandy?" said Julia. Her cheeks were as bright as the sinking sun. But she laughed.

Ellen blinked at Father's rusty chortle. He dipped the pole into the water and glided on downstream without a word in Ellen's direction.

Ouch! Ellen slapped the mosquito and spread her fingers to see if she'd got it.

"Hey, Jack! Willie!" she hollered. "Looky here. A mosquito with wooden teeth!"

The boys laughed. It wasn't her joke. It was Father acting right next to playful. It would shake a laugh out of anyone who knew him.

In the days that followed, Father stayed closer to home than he had in a long while. Ellen thought maybe it was rumors of Indian uprisings keeping him there. One evening, as she was restacking wood she and Willie had knocked over, climbing on the woodpile, playing like they were mountain goats, Julia came around the side of the cabin. Father was sitting on the laundry bench, rubbing tallow into his boots. Julia sat down beside him. Their easy conversation drifted on the evening air as Ellen finished her stacking job.

"Corn's hardly worth shocking," said Father. "It's a wonder we got any crop at all, with it frosting every month of the year."

"What'll you feed the livestock over the winter?"

"Don't plan on wintering much of it. We'll take the hogs up to Galena when I get back from Springfield."

"You're going to Springfield?" said Julia.

Father nodded. "I'll lose money this year. But I've got enough set by to pay Mr. Iles this year's portion of the loan."

"Will you be stopping by to see Clarissa and Washington?" asked Julia.

"I was planning on it. Why?"

"I was thinking of Ellen," said Julia.

"What about Ellen?"

"That you should take her along," said Julia.

"I never saw such a woman for coddling dogs and children," said Father.

"I made her a promise. Or maybe you'd like me to take her myself?"

"Would you two take the payment to Mr. Iles while you're at it?" said Father. "Save me the ride. Fort Dearborn-Springfield Road will take you right there. Keep the gold tucked away in your saddlebag, and don't hug it too close, should you run into anyone along the way. Makes them curious over what you're carrying. And if you find the fords still flooded, why you just . . ."

"Mr. Tandy!" Julia cut in. "Ellen has waited a year and a half without once pleading her cause, and if you don't take her, I will!"

"I believe you," said Father.

His laughter made Ellen's nerves jump. With a trip to Louisa's hanging in the balance, it wasn't a good time to be standing in plain view, listening in on grown-ups. She slipped to the other side of the woodpile and stretched out flat on her face.

"You may as well come, too, have a visit with Clarissa," Father was saying. "Jack says he can keep the boys out of mischief while we're gone."

"You've already talked to Jack?" said Julia, her voice lilting. "Mr. Tandy! You've been planning on taking her all along! Why didn't you say so, instead of provoking me?"

"Where'd be the fun in that?"

Father's chuckle sounded so close, Ellen rolled over and looked up. He was across the woodpile, looking down at her. "'Course maybe Ellen doesn't want to go," he said. "What about it, Ellen? You want to go south, or do you want to stay here and study what's growing under the woodpile?"

"I want to see Louisa," said Ellen.

"All right, then. It's settled. We'll get up early one of these mornings, saddle a couple of horses, and we'll go."

"Julia, too?"

"If you can talk her into it," he said, then donned his hat and walked off toward the barn in his freshly greased boots.

Ellen could barely contain her excitement. She was going to see Louisa before the snow flew! She knocked over a corner stack, circling to thank Julia.

Julie patted her hand. "Thank your father, he's the one who made the plans."

"Because you wanted him to."

"No, Ellen. It had nothing to do with me. He'd already made up his mind to take you."

Ellen could see Julia believed what she was saying. But that didn't make it so. Julia made a difference with Father, whether she knew it or not.

Chapter Thirteen

"Have you ever seen a medicine show?" asked Silas.

"No," said Willie.

"Me, either," said Ellen.

"I did. It was in Cincinnati," said Silas.

They were sitting on the split-rail fence behind the pole barn, waiting for Julia to call them in for lunch. Ellen didn't know what a medicine show was. But she wouldn't give Silas the satisfaction of asking.

Silas's whip sang as he knocked a grasshopper off a seed head a few feet away. "This man was selling stuff in a bottle. Supposed to cure whatever ails you." He flicked a ladybug off a grass stem and said to Ellen, "Let's see you do that."

"Don't want to. I like ladybugs."

"You just can't do it, is all," said Silas with a baiting grin.

"Could if wanted to."

"Dare you," he said, offering her his whip.

Ellen pushed it away and resisted the urge to push him off the fence while she was at it. They were leaving in the morning and she wasn't going to give Father a reason to change his mind about taking her to Louisa's house.

"All right, then, how about the spider there?" said

Silas. He pointed out a lacy web strung between rails.

"Spiders eat bugs that damage crops."

"What about grasshoppers?" asked Silas.

"No, they eat crops. Don't you know anything?"

"I know I can snag that chip and not even graze your shoulder."

"You're the one with the chip on your shoulder," said Ellen, glowering.

"Am not."

"Are, too."

"What's a medicine show?" inserted Willie.

"A fast talker, using slick stunts to sell whatever it is he's selling. This fella said he used to have weak eyes," Silas went on with his story. "But then he started taking this medicine—I can't remember what he called it. Dr. Something-Something's Miracle Something. Anyway, he said it made him keen eyed as a hawk. Then he drank a swallow and commenced to show how good his eyes were."

"How?" asked Willie.

"With a bullwhip. He took a deck of cards from his pocket and had a pretty lady hold up the ace of hearts. He hit that card with his whip, took out the heart, clean as a whistle."

"What else could he do?"

"He knocked the ash off another fellow's cigar. 'Course there's nothing to that. Want me to show you?"

Willie's eyebrows arched. "Can you?"

"Sure. And I don't need to take medicine, either. Stand up there on the stump and I'll show you."

"Where am I going to get a cigar?"

"A rolled-up leaf would do just as good," said Silas.

"Don't do it, Willie," warned Ellen. "He'll put your eye out."

"Wouldn't try it if I couldn't do it," said Silas. "We'll show her, won't we, Willie?"

"We?" Ellen scowled, arms crossed. "Willie's got no part in it, except a sitting-duck part."

"It'll be all right, Ellie. Ready?" said Willie, and hopped off the fence, a rolled leaf in his mouth.

Ellen watched him take his stance, then slapped her hands over her eyes as Silas's whip snaked toward him.

"Looky there!"

"I told you," said Silas as Willie held up a stub of rolled leaf. "And scaredy-cat Ellen missed it."

"Didn't, either. I was looking."

"You were not."

"Was, too. Between my fingers."

"We could do it again, if you want to see without your fingers in the way."

"Sure. We can do that," agreed Willie.

Ellen couldn't bear seeing Silas swing that whip at Willie again. She jumped off the fence. "No fair. It's my turn."

"You sure?"

"Wouldn't have said it if I wasn't," Ellen bumped Willie out of the line of fire. "'Course if you miss, you have to hold the leaf and let *me* try."

"In my mouth?"

"Yes, in your mouth."

Second thoughts sent the sneaky grin limping right off Silas's face. Ellen held her breath. But at length, he shrugged, and said, "Fair enough. Grab a leaf."

Ellen shouted down the voice in her head and rolled the leaf between her hands. She turned so she was standing with her left side facing him.

"You're stretching your neck like Matilda reaching for a bug," scoffed Silas. "Stand up straight, I'm not going to hit you!"

"You do and you'll be everlasting sorry," Ellen said around the leaf. The veins in Silas's wrist stood out in bold relief as he gathered the whip and tightened his grip.

"Ready?"

"Just do it!"

At the last millisecond, Ellen's nerve wavered. She twitched in the wrong direction. The whip stung like a hornet. Her hand flew to her cheek and came away bloody.

"You *hit* me!"

"I didn't mean to. You moved!"

Ellen charged and knocked him to the ground. But before she could pound him, Father snagged her by the skirt tail and hauled her to her feet. Silas turned white and rolled up like a porcupine. In one stride, one jerk, Father had the whip.

"How'd you like it if *I* hit *you*?"

Silas covered himself with upraised arms and wailed. His shrieks raised the hair on Ellen's neck, and Father's dander with it.

"Stop that caterwauling!" he thundered, and would have snatched him to his feet, except Julia got there first.

"Get away!" Her cold warning cut the air. "Don't touch him!"

"Go back to the house, Julia. I'll handle this."

Julia dropped to the ground and flung her arms around Silas. "It's all right. No one's going to hurt you," she said over and over again.

Father dropped the whip and tipped Ellen's chin as if to defend his anger. His hands were rough and smelled of horseflesh. But it wasn't his hard fingers on her bloody cheek that made Ellen flinch. It was Silas's wails.

She couldn't look at him, humiliating himself there on the ground. Or Julia, upholding his behavior. Or Father, an unwitting participant, too. As was she. The twinge of conscience told her as much.

Julia snatched up the discarded whip, and with a defiant look, gave it to Silas. "Go to the shed, Silas. Wait there until I come for you."

Silas's weeping quieted. He hugged the whip close and did as he was told.

"A word with you in the house, Mr. Tandy," said Julia, her voice thin and tight.

"Wash your face in the spring," Father said to Ellen.

Without turning back, Julia said, "Yarrow will stop the bleeding."

Father followed her to the house, his stride tearing up the grass.

"Does it hurt, Ellie?" whispered Willie.

Something hurt. She should have spoken up. Even now she could tell them it was an accident, her fault as much as Silas's. Or was it too late? As the door banged shut behind Father and Julia, fear gripped in the same heart-wild way of the prairie fire months and months ago. The thick log walls couldn't contain their quarrel:

"Is this the way you handle him?" demanded Father. "You *did* say you'd handle him, that I didn't have the patience for it."

"You've proved my point."

"I wasn't going to hit him."

"Forgive me then for not waiting to see," Julia's stilted voice crowded out the apology.

"Ellen? You're supposed to wash at the spring," whispered Willie.

"Shh!"

"I can tell you what *didn't* happen," Julia interrupted whatever it was Ellen had missed while shrugging Willie's hand off her arm. "Silas didn't hit Ellen on purpose. I know my son. You don't, and you never will, not if you continue to compare him to Jack."

"Jack? He's got nothing to do with this!"

"Silas isn't Jack."

"I don't expect him to be."

"Don't you? Then how is it you see his weaknesses but never his strengths? You have, from the day we arrived. You treat him like he isn't worth teaching!"

"Make up your mind, Julia. Do you want me to let

him grow like a weed? Or do you want me to take a hand with him?"

"I want him to grow up straight and strong and sound on the inside. How is that going to happen if you can't hold on to your temper?"

"Me? What about you wrapping him in cotton batting? If you want a man, then treat him like one!"

"He isn't a man, he's a boy!"

"He'll stay one, too, unless you expect more of him. Send him with Jack and me when we drive hogs north next month. Let him use that whip for the purpose intended."

"As punishment? Or to teach him?" asked Julia.

Father cursed the way he did when the ax was dull or wolves killed sheep or the chimney was slow to draw and smoked up the cabin.

"We're going back to Springfield, Mr. Tandy," said Julia, matching his heat without swear words.

"What are you saying?"

"You heard me. This isn't working. I've been deceiving myself, thinking it could."

The door slammed as only Father could slam it. Willie ducked for cover. The faint hope of mending what she had broken kept Ellen in place as Father rounded the cabin. His eyes burned like coals beneath ashes.

"We're leaving for Springfield, Ellen. Get yourself ready if you want to go."

"Now?"

"Yes, now."

"I don't want her to go," said Ellen, throat hurting.

"You can't make somebody stay where they don't want to be."

Ellen's tears spilled free as Father tilted her face and looked at the gash on her cheek. "Why haven't you washed this?"

"He didn't do it on purpose."

"He shouldn't have done it at all. Wash your face and get ready to go." Father released her chin and strode out to the pasture to catch the horses.

Even as Ellen told herself Julia wouldn't really go, her heart ticked down to disaster.

Chapter Fourteen

They set out within the hour, Father driving the wagon. Julia rode in back with Silas. Ellen followed on Gertie. The packing had been hasty, and Julia was bent on redoing the job. The canvas flap was open. As the wagon bumped southbound over the Springfield-Fort Dearborn Road, Ellen could see Silas helping her wrap dishes and tucking them in with her quilts.

Hearing a sound behind them, Ellen turned to see Wolf following them. She tried to make him go back, but he wouldn't. Father tried, too. Wolf dropped back but kept following.

Father set his jaw and ignored him. The first creek that needed crossing, Julia made Silas help her get Wolf into the wagon. The creek was full of debris from all the flooding. It was just the first of numerous treacherous crossings.

Ellen didn't see any wildlife, not even a squirrel. But a lot of animal skeletons littered the trail. At one point she saw an eerie white covering blanketing the woodland floor. It was bones from a herd of deer that had been trapped by the deep snow and perished.

The hazardous fordings of creeks and streams slowed them down drastically. Father stopped from time to time to rest the team. Darkness fell, but they didn't stop.

Father left the road and cut across open country where there was no road.

The moon came up, dimly lighting their way over prairie and around tall timber. Ellen couldn't keep her eyes open. Father tied Gertie to the back of the wagon and lifted her up on the seat.

Ellen awakened at daybreak as Father stopped the wagon in front of Uncle Washington and Aunt Clarissa's cabin. She didn't hear Father's explanation. Maybe he didn't make one. Maybe his stern face and Julia's tears told the story without words.

Father fed and watered and rested the horses while Aunt Clarissa served Silas and Ellen from a pot she had left simmering on the fire. Julia had not come in, nor did Father take time to eat.

"I'll be a few days, seeing to business and getting them settled," Ellen heard him say to Aunt Clarissa as he prepared to leave. "Thanks for looking after Ellen."

Ellen's limbs felt heavy and sore. But she followed Father and Silas back to the wagon.

"Sorry, Ellen," said Silas, his voice as still as the dawn.

"Me, too," she whispered back. "Do you think . . ."

But Silas climbed into the back of the wagon without waiting to hear her wishful thinking. Ellen's eyes misted. Father brushed past her, then stopped and turned.

"Seem to recall you were wanting some calico," he said. "Blue, wasn't it?"

Ellen wanted to tell him she had two dresses that

Julia had made her, that dresses weren't what she needed. But, already, he was mounting the wagon seat, giving her no chance to undo the damage she and Silas had done.

Julia climbed out to hug Ellen good-bye. "Help Willie with his reading," she said, and stroked her hair. "I left something for you. Something I was going to give you on your birthday. I hope you like it."

Ellen was too full of tears to ask what it was.

Julia kissed Ellen and climbed into the wagon again.

"What happened to your cheek?" asked Aunt Clarissa as they walked back to the cabin together.

"Silas's whip." A sob caught in Ellen's throat. Fresh tears washed over the tender stripe. "I wanted calico and Julia c-came. N-now I want Julia and Father's bringing me blue calico!"

"There, there. You're tuckered out, and here's Louisa, just waking up," said Aunt Clarissa.

Louisa stumbled to the cabin door, rubbing the sleep from her eyes.

"Ellen! Am I dreaming?"

"It's her, and she's pert near asleep on her feet," said Aunt Clarissa."

"Oh, don't go to sleep, Ellie," pleaded Louisa, throwing her arms around her. "You've got to see baby George! Areanna's as jealous as a cat. Isn't she, Mama? She wanted a baby sister, and she hasn't got over it yet. Ellie!" Louisa ground to a halt. "What's wrong?"

"Shush, Louisa, and get dressed," said Aunt Clarissa. "Your dad can use some help with the chores."

"But I'm hungry. Besides, Ellen's crying," protested Louisa. "Ellie never cries."

"Nonsense," said Aunt Clarissa. "Everyone cries. Go on, now. The sooner you finish, the sooner you'll have breakfast."

Reluctantly, Louisa dressed and went outside. Aunt Clarissa tucked Ellen into her own bed and questioned her closely. Ellen was too spent to hold back. She repeated every searing word that had flown between Julia and Father.

The ropes undergirding the straw tick creaked as Aunt Clarissa sat down and gathered Ellen in her arms. "Here I've been worried about Indians and cholera and every disaster imaginable and a whip is Gil's undoing."

"We sh-shouldn't've played that g-game," whimpered Ellen.

"This isn't your fault," said Aunt Clarissa, with her comforting aroma of rosewater, baby burps, and wood smoke. "Don't go blaming yourself or Silas, either."

Uncle Washington strode through the door with Louisa at his heels. "So what happened?" he asked Aunt Clarissa.

"Julia's a she bear with a wounded cub, and Gil's got too much temper. That's the long and short if it," said Aunt Clarissa. "That, and pride."

"Wish I'd f-fed that wh-whip to the pigs a long time ago," said Ellen brokenly.

"Fretting won't help," said Aunt Clarissa, smoothing Ellen's hair. "Let's pray your daddy and Julia have enough sense to work it out on the road to Springfield before they do something they'll both regret."

Aunt Clarissa did the praying, then dried Ellen's tears on her apron.

"Here's Georgie," said Louisa, plucking the sleeping baby from the sugar trough. "Wanna see?"

In the past, brothers were about the only thing Ellen had had that Louisa didn't. Now Louisa had a brother, and she had lost one, and a second mother as well. Ellen's eyes burned as she touched his pudgy hand. He was dimpled and plump and pretty and perfect. Like everything else in Louisa's life.

It was a long day of watching for Ellen. Waiting to see if Father and Julia would work out their differences, and turn back. Now, as Aunt Clarissa bustled about, warming water and washing the children for bed, hope burned out.

After months of waiting to be with Louisa, all she wanted was to be in her own home under Julia's red quilt, while Father and the boys settled down to sleep in the next room.

A squirrel scampered over the roof. Little George whimpered. An owl shrieked. But as Ellen drifted off to sleep, the sounds shifted and blended into Silas's shrieks. In her dream, Father wasn't just standing over him with the whip in hand. He was using it.

She awoke in a cold sweat, and crowded closer to Louisa.

Chapter Fifteen

The next morning, Ellen set off for New Salem with Louisa's family. The village was scattered over a woodsy bluff three miles from Uncle Washington's farm. Aunt Clarissa had spun wool and woven linsey-woolsy to trade. Uncle Washington brought along tools to be sharpened and corn to be milled. Areanna and baby Georgie rode on the horse with him. Ellen and Louisa walked with Aunt Clarissa.

"Sorry-looking corn," said Uncle Wash as they traveled past neighboring fields. Late going in and the frost caught it before it could ripen."

"I've never seen such a year for weather." Aunt Clarissa sighed.

"Georgie's growing better than anything on the place," said Uncle Wash.

"Me, too," said Areanna. "I'm growing even gooder."

"Tall as a blue willow," chimed Louisa, grinning. Yesterday, she told Ellen about the snowy January day that Georgie was born, and how she had pounded corn and carded wool all the winter long so her mama could have blue willow dishes. But Aunt Clarissa was taking her time, making up her mind.

As they neared a flush of autumn trees, Uncle Washington winked and teased, "You and Sam Hill going to come to terms today, Clarissa?"

She sniffed and replied, "His isn't the only store in the village."

"Maybe you'd find Mr. Offutt's young clerk easier to bargain with," said Uncle Washington. "He's as tall and rawboned as a bare tree, but folks find him fair in his dealings."

"I'm tall as a bear tree," said Areanna. She growled and stretched her chin, trying to look tall as she rode along behind Uncle Washington. "See?"

Uncle Washington was too busy teasing Aunt Clarissa to pay her any mind. They reached some leg-stretching country and saved their breath for climbing. The rutted track wound through the trees to the village at the top of the bluff.

Ellen heard the ring of the smithy's hammer as Uncle Washington tied his horse in front of the blacksmith shop. He handed Georgie down to Louisa, turned Areanna over to Aunt Clarissa, and unstrapped his froe.

"Georgie and I will be at the mill, when you finish your errands."

"What's about me?" demanded Areanna, hands on her hips as Uncle Washington strode into the shop with Georgie on his arm.

"It's hot and dirty and icky sticky in there and you get cinders in your eyes," said Louisa quickly. "We'll have more fun shopping dishes."

Areanna gave the shop one last puckered glance, then pranced stiff legged to the road. "Walk like trees, Weezie."

"It's her favorite game," explained Louisa. She giggled and added, "Just do it."

Areanna nearly walked into the path of an oxen team. Aunt Clarissa tugged her out of harm's way and chided, "Watch where you're going, Areanna. Louisa, don't let go of her hand again."

Ellen took Areanna's other hand. They scuffed through the crisp autumn leaves and up the road to Mr. Hill's store.

"You girls can sit here on the step and wait," said Aunt Clarissa, opening the door.

"I want to go!" cried Areanna.

So do I! thought Ellen. She hadn't been in a store since Mama died.

But Aunt Clarissa didn't even look back. Louisa plunked down on the step with Areanna and pointed out a woolly worm crawling over the hitching post. It was moving at about the same speed as the tears spilling down Areanna's cheeks.

"Oohh!" squealed Louisa, pointing at Areanna's face. "There's a woolly worm rolling down your cheek."

Louisa crawled her fingers down Areanna's face and sang:

"Teeny-weeny woolly worm, woozles up your face,
Splash comes a teardrop and washes him away."

"Come back, woolly worm. Make him come back," said Areanna.

"Can't. You washed him out."

Areanna rubbed her eyes with her fists. "Make him come back."

"Teeny-weeny woolly worm, woozles up your face,
Glimmer comes a smile and jollies up the place."

Areanna giggled and stuck her cheek closer to
Louisa's walking fingers. "Do it again, Weezie."

Louisa sang and walked her fingers all over
Areanna's freckled face. Ellen couldn't help smiling.
Louisa could cheer anyone up. They didn't wait long.

"I believe I'll look around before I make up my
mind, Mr. Hill," said Aunt Clarissa as she let herself out.

The Offutt store was at the east end of town on the
way to the mill. Louisa and Ellen followed Aunt Clarissa
inside, after promising to keep Areanna between them.
There was a fellow lolled back on a chair in the corner,
reading a book.

He greeted them, then ducked his head again and
went on reading.

Aunt Clarissa wandered down the length of one
wall. She picked up a blue plate, turned it over, looked
at the back, then returned it to the shelf. She did the
same with a plate that was plain, like the jars and jugs
on the next shelf up.

"Oh, no! Not those," whispered Louisa for Ellen's
ears alone.

"What's the matter with 'em?" Ellen whispered
back.

"I want pretty ones. Like Julia's," said Louisa. "I
hope she gets a teapot, too."

Ellen didn't like thinking about Julia's teapot, broken in the fire. She supposed the spring floods had
strung the pieces hither and yon.

Aunt Clarissa put the glazed pottery plate back and crossed to the yard goods shelf. She singled out a deep blue piece with tiny white curved specks on it.

"How much is this blue cotton, Mr. . . ."

"Lincoln, ma'am. Abe Lincoln." He lay a piece of stove wood across the book to mark his page and stood up as Aunt Clarissa introduced herself.

Ellen dropped her head back, looking up at him. He had a long face and deep-set eyes, a large nose, and the biggest ears she had ever seen on a human being. He squinted one eye, scratched his head, and tipped his head back, as if seeking the price on the ceiling. His boatman's cap tipped and fell to the floor.

Areanna scooped it up. She looked up and up and up. "Are you a tree?" she asked.

Aunt Clarissa's face turned bright red. "Areanna!"

"Is he?" persisted Areanna.

The man laughed as he retrieved his hat. "If I were, what kind do you reckon I'd be?"

"A bear tree," said Areanna. She wrinkled up her face and made growly noises.

"Not a bear tree, a *bare* tree," said Louisa. "One with no leaves. That's what Daddy meant when he said . . ."

"Louisa!"

Aunt Clarissa's sharp warning stopped the words in time.

"Do bears grow from bear trees?" asked Areanna.

"Only in pinchin' times," said Mr. Lincoln.

Aunt Clarissa smiled as if he'd told a joke. Ellen

traded glances with Louisa. Louisa shrugged to say she didn't get it, either.

"I can walk like a tree," chirped Areanna.

"Walk like a lady instead, and take yourself out to the front step to wait, please." Aunt Clarissa spoke so firmly that Areanna didn't have to be told twice. "Go with her, Louisa. Now about the cloth, Mr. Lincoln."

Ellen meant to follow. But she couldn't pull herself away from all the geegaws on the store shelves. Aunt Clarissa haggled, trying to get the most for her winter's work. Mr. Lincoln expected as much. Ellen noticed how his eyes strayed to his book on the chair, and how quick he was to let Aunt Clarissa talk him down. Must be a real good book!

He measured off an equal amount of white fabric, using the brass tacks that marked off a yard on the counter while Aunt Clarissa puttered about the store, replenishing her tea supply and a few other items.

Mr. Lincoln did some ciphering, made change, and ambled back to his book.

"Mama! You forgot the dishes," cried Louisa as Ellen followed Aunt Clarissa into the autumn sunshine.

"I didn't forget a thing," said Aunt Clarissa stoutly.

"But we planned and planned for dishes. It's all we talked about the whole while you were spinning and weaving!"

"It's all you talked about. I've been wanting to make an Orange Peel quilt for a long time now."

"Orange? That's blue."

"Orange Peel is the pattern," said Aunt Clarissa. "A

body can make it any color she chooses. The blue's about the same color as those dishes, and we'll have the joy of putting ourselves into it."

"But I wanted dishes!" cried Louisa, with quick tears.

"A quilt's more lasting. It'll warm us while we're making it, and for years and years to come, too. Say, Louisa! Let's stitch your name on the border, shall we?"

"Mine, too," said Areanna, taking in every word. "But not Georgie!"

"I don't reckon Georgie cares one way or the other," said Aunt Clarissa, taking Areanna by the hand.

Areanna skipped along, pleased as could be. But to Ellen's surprise, Louisa sulked all the way down the bluff to the mill where they were to meet Uncle Washington. It was a new and not so sunny side to her cousin.

There were horses tied along the bank near the mill at the bottom of the hill. Uncle Washington was just one in a long line of folks waiting to have his corn ground. Aunt Clarissa ambled over to a group of women on the bank of the Sangamon. Areanna curled up on her lap and napped while the ladies chatted of quilts and counterpanes and who was sick and who was courting and who had skipped town without paying their bills.

Ellen sat with them until Louisa tired of pouting and suggested they gather autumn leaves and acorns. They loosened the caps on the acorns and pretended they were gentlemen dolls who took off their hats to bow.

It was a long wait for Uncle Wash, and an even

longer walk home. The sun was setting by the time they reached the cabin.

"You're tuckered out, Ellie. Rest until supper," said Aunt Clarissa. She turned down the worn quilt on her bed.

Ellen awakened a while later and struggled to place the voices in the fire-lit cabin. Then Louisa giggled and she remembered where she was. Georgie cried on Aunt Clarissa's shoulder while Uncle Wash strode over to answer a knock at the door.

"It's him! It's him! It's the bear tree!" squealed Areanna.

Ellen recognized him, too. It was Mr. Lincoln from the store. He bent his tall frame as he came through the door.

"This is my wife, Clarissa. Clarissa, this is Abe Lincoln I was telling you about."

"We met in the store today," said Aunt Clarissa.

"Yes, ma'am," said Mr. Lincoln. "It came to me after you left that I'd shortchanged you six and a quarter cents. I couldn't sit on my backbone resting, until I'd set it straight."

"You walked all the way out here for that?" said Uncle Wash as the coins changed hands.

"I'd have been here sooner, but I had to wait until customers cleared out to close the store," replied Mr. Lincoln.

"Wish you hadn't put yourself out that way. You could have squared it with us, next time we came to town."

"That would have been plenty soon enough," chimed Aunt Clarissa.

"As long as you're here, can you sit a spell?" invited Uncle Wash.

"Don't mind if I do."

Mr. Lincoln's trouser legs climbed as he folded his lean frame into the offered chair. At ease with George's whimpers, Areanna's bear growls, and Louisa's lively chatter, he accepted Aunt Clarissa's invitation to share potluck.

Ellen's thoughts drifted in and out of Mr. Lincoln and Uncle Wash's talk of crops and weather and folks coming to fill up Illinois. After dinner, she helped Louisa and Aunt Clarissa clear away the leavings while Mr. Lincoln gave Areanna a pony ride on his bony knee. They were soon on the best of terms.

"Bye-bye, bear tree," she called, and waved when he finally bid them good night.

Aunt Clarissa chided, but Uncle Wash laughed and scratched his head and said, "He stands pretty tall, doesn't he, Areanna?"

"Honest men always do," said Aunt Clarissa.

Chapter Sixteen

The next morning when the chores were done, Ellen and Louisa wandered down to Rock Creek and played with acorns and arrowheads. Louisa pretended the acorn caps were teacups and complained some more over Aunt Clarissa's poor trade.

"The quilt will be pretty," said Ellen. "You're lucky."

"Lucky? It isn't even red, it's blue."

Ellen arranged arrowheads to look like stars.

"Pretend it's a star quilt," said Louisa. "We're having Sunday dinner on the grounds."

"Julia and I could have made a quilt. If she'd stayed."

"Cream and sugar?"

"Maple sugar." Ellen played along.

"Think Julia'll come back?"

Ellen wanted to, but couldn't. Julia felt as lost to her as Mama. Had she been right in the beginning, thinking it was a grown-up game of pretend? The arrowheads glittered, starlike, as her eyes misted.

"Father didn't act married," she said, and wiped her dripping nose. "Julia, either."

"They were," said Louisa. "I was there when Preacher Berry said the words."

If words weren't enough to marry them, then what about rafts and snakes and wolves? What about dead sheep and a wounded dog? Onion milk? A lost ax? Indian scares? Deep snows and high water? What would it have taken to keep them from falling apart at the crack of a whip?

Crowding out the thought, Ellen told Louisa about running from the ground fire. She could still hear the sound of Julia's teapot breaking as Gertie threw her. Louisa spilled acorns every which way as she leaped to her feet to act it out.

"I'll be Julia, you be you. Pretend this is my horse," said Louisa. She mounted a log and "rode" to the rescue while Ellen ran from smoke and fire.

"And he bucks me off! See his eyes roll! He's wild with fear!" Louisa screamed. She flung her bag of arrow-heads in the air and tumbled off the log, then leaped to her feet, squealing, "Catch her, catch her, catch her!"

Ellen snagged the reins of the make-believe horse.

"Not my teapot! My teapot, my poor precious teapot!" squealed Louisa. She scrambled in the leaves, as if trying to put the teapot together again.

Ellen didn't spoil good drama by telling Louisa it hadn't happened like that. That Julia hadn't gone back for the pieces, or even shed a tear. Nor did she mention Julia hugging her leg, hugging Willie, too. But it comforted her, remembering. Julia had risked life and limb, coming for them once.

Maybe Louisa was right. Maybe Julia would come back again. She'd keep praying and hoping and watching.

After lunch, while the little ones napped, Aunt Clarissa spread her store-bought cloth over the bed. Ellen ran her hand over the blue. "It's like a starry night."

"It is, isn't it?" said Aunt Clarissa. "See there, Louisa? Ellen likes it."

"It isn't dishes," said Louisa.

"My neighbor has an Orange Peel quilt pieced in browns and yellows," Aunt Clarissa talked right over her. "I drew off a pattern." She retrieved a scrap of fabric cut in an eight-inch square and a smaller scrap cut in a half-moon shape.

"Wipe the table, Louisa. Ellen, prop the door open. We need all the light we can get. We'll have to be very careful, now. The secret to a well-made quilt is in the preparation."

It rained off and on over the next five days. When the last half-moon shaped piece was cut, Aunt Clarissa gave into their coaxing and spread a corner of the bed in blue-and-white pieces so they could see what the quilt would look like when it was sewed together.

Ellen studied it from every angle. There was something so familiar about it. Then it hit her. "It's like Julia's quilt!" she cried. "Remember, Louisa?"

"The red one!" Louisa clapped her hands, cheering their discovery. "The one she called Robbing Peter to Pay Paul."

"I like the name Orange Peel better," said Ellen. "She'll come back."

"Lou," murmured Aunt Clarissa, as if Louisa had offered her a bone with no meat.

"She might!" defended Louisa.

"Pick up the pieces if you're finished," said Aunt Clarissa.

Later that afternoon, Ellen's seesawing hopes and fears touched ground as Father stopped Julia's wagon at the edge of the yard. Gertie and one of Julia's horses were hitched to it. But Julia wasn't with him, and neither was Silas.

Ellen tried to ask, but couldn't. "Where's Wolf?" she said instead.

"He stayed in Springfield with Julia." Father set the brake and swung down off the wagon seat.

"How long can you stay?" asked Aunt Clarissa, when she and Uncle Wash had welcomed him.

"Just for the night. Trails are heavy with mud. It'll take us twice as long to get home with that wagon as it would riding Gertie."

"What're you doing with her wagon?" asked Uncle Wash.

"I bought it. She needed the money more than she needed the wagon," said Father.

"What she needs is you," said Aunt Clarissa.

Father didn't answer.

"Go back and set things right with her, can't you?" urged Aunt Clarissa.

"She knows the way," Father replied. "At least, she ought to. She's been over the road twice."

"So have you," said Aunt Clarissa, her voice as tart as a gooseberry. "So have you."

Ellen knew by Father's grim mouth that Aunt Clarissa was wasting her breath. *Did he miss Julia? Or was it the loss of his sheep dog and the expense of a wagon in a year of failed crops that etched stern shadows and lines on his face?*

The next morning, Father thanked Aunt Clarissa for looking after Ellen. Ellen hugged everyone good-bye, and clambered aboard the wagon beside Father.

Aunt Clarissa shaded her eyes, looking up at Father. "Will we see you in the spring?"

"I'll be stopping by the third week in May when I come to pay off the rest of my note," said Father.

"Can Ellie come, too?" asked Louisa.

Father shook the lines and chirruped to the team without answering.

"Can she?" cried Louisa, keeping pace as the wagon rolled out of the yard.

"Depends on how things go," said Father.

Ellen knew how things would go. They would go as they had gone before Julia came. Father would bury himself in his work, expecting of them no more than he expected of himself. Which was a lot. What was it Aunt Clarissa had said to her and Louisa yesterday? *Pick up the pieces if you're finished.*

It seemed to apply to the family they might have been. The pieces were raw edged. They gouged Ellen all the way home, then cut her afresh when she found what Julia had left behind for her.

It was her red wedding quilt. Worn out from the trip, Ellen wrapped herself in it and cried.

They had been home only a few days when Father hired a neighbor to look after the place, then left Ellen and Willie with Mrs. Kelly while he and Jack and Mr. Kelly drove hogs north to Galena.

Winter set on shortly after they returned. It was not nearly so harsh as the previous winter had been. But it seemed even longer and bleaker. Even the stories grew stale.

"One time Tee," Jack would begin. When he finished, they would laugh. But without heart, like when you try to talk and listen at the same time, and end up not knowing what you've heard or half of what you've said.

Maybe it was finished between Father and Julia, but that didn't keep them from missing her. It was different from the pain of losing Mama. Nothing they could have done would have prevented that loss. "A treasure laid up in Heaven," that's what the circuit preacher had said about Mama.

Julia was a treasure, too, lost to them in a way that ought never to have happened. Was that what made it so hard for Ellen to accept? Or was it the fear that she bore some of the responsibility?

One blustery day, Ellen walked out to her mother's grave. She crouched down in a patch of dirty snow and whispered, "God, would you please send Julia back?

Jack's grumpy and I'm sad and Willie's sad. And no matter how stubborn he's being, Father wouldn't turn her away if she came back."

Ellen trailed her fingers through the snow. Maybe she shouldn't have said that part right here at Mama's grave. If Mama were here, she sure wouldn't want Father loving someone else. But Mama wasn't here. She'd done her work and gone home to her Maker. It was a good job she had done. Good enough to make them all want to fill the empty place she had left. There was nothing disloyal in their loving Julia. She wished she had realized that sooner.

"Anyway, if You could give us all another chance, I'll be nicer to Silas. Honest, I will."

Spring came at last, melting the snow, swelling the creeks and streams, and making the prairie bloom. With the blooming came ominous news: Black Hawk had crossed to the east side of the Mississippi, leading one thousand Indians, women, and children among them.

The news came as the community gathered in a neighbor's cabin for services led by the young circuit preacher. According to him, Black Hawk claimed his people were moving north to Wisconsin to take up possession of hunting grounds left behind by the Pottawotamies. There had been no violence. Yet Governor Reynolds saw Black Hawk's movement as a violation of the treaty and a threat to the frontier. He issued a call to arms.

"The volunteers are to rendezvous on the twenty-second of April," said the preacher.

"That's the day after tomorrow," said Jack.

Moments later, Ellen saw Jack follow Reverend Crissey into the yard where his horse was tethered. She knew as the two men stood talking beneath the trees that Jack intended to answer the call. She was right. Not even Father could dissuade Jack from enlisting with his friend Tee.

Ellen had just finished the evening milking when Jack said good-bye. Father was in the pasture, saddling Gertie. Jack strode in that direction. Their voices carried to Ellen.

"I'm leaving now, Father."

Father had his back to Jack. He didn't answer.

"I was hoping you'd shake my hand and wish me well."

"I was hoping I hadn't raised boys who couldn't think for themselves."

Color swept up Jack's neck and face at Father's words. The silence stretched until it made Ellen's ears hurt from listening so hard.

"Guess I'll head on over to Tee's," Jack said at length. "We've got a long walk ahead of us."

"I got no quarrel with you following your conscience, if you've thought this thing through," said Father. "But if you're going because Tee's going, and you fall in with some more like you, out to whoop Indians and be heroes, you'll soon have a bloody mess on your hands."

"It's only thirty days, Father."

"You don't know much about Indians and even less about war."

Jack shifted his weight and tugged at his hat. "Guess we'll learn together."

"Yup, you will, sure enough. I hope you don't get yourselves scalped, whetting your horns," said Father.

Ellen put her hands over her ears. Jack retraced his steps to her side. His choppy stride reminded her of shaking your hand when you'd burned it stirring the pot. He bumped the milk bucket with his foot, sloshing milk up over the sides. She lifted her wet face in silent entreaty.

"There you go, crying over spilt milk," said Jack, and laughed when Ellen kicked him.

Willie came running from the cabin. He plowed into Jack and knocked him to the ground for one last wrestling hug. Ellen piled on, and before they were done, they had spilled the milk for real.

"Now see what you've done," said Jack, rolling to his feet to dust off his trousers.

"You started it," said Ellen.

Jack clapped her on the back, knocked the dents out of his hat, and cocked it low over his eye, head of the pack again. "Come on, you two. Walk me halfway to Tee's."

"Guess you won't be needing Gertie, then."

Ellen turned to see Father leading his saddled horse. Jack's face twitched as Father gave him the reins.

"Try and get her back to me in one piece," growled Father.

Jack gave a mute nod and thanked him and swung into the saddle. He would have ridden away, except that Father reached up and clasped his ankle with a hand as leathery as the boot. They traded a long wordless gaze. Then Jack swallowed hard and reached down and shook Father's hand.

Ellen and Willie called good-byes and raised their hands. But Jack wheeled away on Gertie without looking back.

Just like Father.

Chapter Seventeen

Jack's departure left Father shorthanded. The plowing and planting and other spring work would begin just as soon as the ground dried. Corn for planting was a worry, too. It was scarce, due to last year's failed crop. Father had fed what corn he had to stock over the past winter. He was hoping to buy seed corn while he was in Springfield to pay off his debt. But with the whole frontier holding its breath over the Indian situation, he was reluctant to leave Ellen and Willie with neighbors.

"I doubt if there's any real danger this far south," he said one evening a week after Jack's departure. "But on the other hand, if there's trouble up north, the Indians could scatter all over the state. Guess I'd rest easier having you with me."

"You mean we get to go to Louisa's?" cried Ellen.

"First things first. I'll take care of business in Springfield," said Father. "We'll stop by Clarissa's on the way home."

It was the brightest bit of news to come Ellen's way in a long while. Willie was excited, too. He hadn't been to Aunt Clarissa's since Mama died. Father said they would go the third week in May.

Meanwhile, Ellen marked off the days of Jack's enlistment on the same length of wall where she had counted snows and Silas had counted snakes. They were anxious days, for there was no word from Jack. Rumors drifted back that the volunteers were moving up the Rock River Valley in search of Black Hawk and his band.

"There's a lot of tall timber and sloughs up that way, and the Indians know the country," Father said one evening when their nearest neighbor, Jeb Thompson, stopped by to return a borrowed tool.

"Black Hawk pushes, he'll get pushed back," said Mr. Thompson. "We got numbers on our side."

"If the governor gets the regular army in on time, we do," said Father. "In the meantime, our boys are sitting on a powder keg. They'd best sit tight until they've figured out Black Hawk's intentions."

"We can take 'em, Gil." Jeb shot a stream of tobacco toward the weeds and added, "If he sparks a war, he'll find out right quick how much he has to lose."

Life, that's what. Ellen shivered and prayed for Jack.

The evening before they were to leave for Springfield, Father let the fire burn down almost to ash. He pushed the remaining ashes and coals to one side, then ducked into the fireplace, reached up into the chimney, removed a loose stone, and withdrew a smoke-darkened deerskin pouch from its hiding place. The pouch contained gold coins, earnings from last fall's hog drive. He packed it into his saddlebags along with the bull's tongue plowshares and some provisions for the trip. Only one horse remained in the pasture, the mare he had bought from Julia. He saddled it and rode over to Jeb Thompson's to make arrangement for the livestock while they were away. It was dark when he returned.

"Something's come up," Father said, sorting through the provisions by the door. "We'll have to put off our trip to Springfield for a few days."

"Why? What's wrong?" cried Ellen, catching his alarm.

"I ran into a courier limping down the road. Said he was taking a message north to General Atkinson when his horse threw him and ran off."

Ellen's pulse quickened at Father's grim demeanor. General Atkinson was a familiar name to her. He was in charge at Fort Armstrong where Father had taken cattle. *That's where all the Indian trouble was!*

"What are you going to do?" she asked.

"Carry the message," said Father.

"But the Indians are up north," cried Willie as Father flung the bull's tongue plowshares to one side and returned the gold to its hiding place.

"Do you have to go?" whispered Ellen.

"No," said Father. "But if I don't, a lot of good men may die."

Like Jack. Worries skittered like mice in a granary. But Ellen beat them back and followed Father and Willie outside.

"Jeb's going to come for you as soon as him and Cora get the courier doctored and settled in," said Father.

"We can walk over by ourselves," said Ellen.

"No," said Father as he secured his saddlebags to the

horse. "I don't want you missing each other in the dark."

Fresh chills fanned over Ellen's belly at Father's uncharacteristic caution. As he swung into the saddle, she thought of him sending Jack all the way to the mill when he wasn't any older than she was now. Springfield, too.

"Jeb and Cora have got a brood of their own. So you two stay out from underfoot as best you can," said Father as he started away.

To Ellen's surprise, he flung them a backward glance. *Had he changed his mind?* But, no. He waved and urged his horse into a trot.

Ellen squared her shoulders so Willie wouldn't guess at her shrinking courage as the dark woods swallowed Father whole. "Come on," she said. "We'll light a candle and read while we wait for Mr. Thompson."

It was crowded at Jeb and Cora Thompson's cabin. They had five children, all of them younger than Willie. But the courier Father had replaced was gone by the time Ellen and Willie arrived.

"Where'd he go?" Jeb asked Cora.

"He was set on getting back to the gov'nor so he'd know he'd failed through no fault of his own," said Cora from her spinning wheel.

"Wouldn't call it a failure," said Jeb. "Not with Gil riding in his place. He'll get the message through if anyone can."

"That's what I told him. But nothing I said could keep him from stewing," said Cora. "Bad piece of luck, losing his horse. He'd best be giving that thigh wound of his some rest and attention."

"I'd hate to walk all the way to Vandalia on a gimpy leg," said Jeb, and slumped down on the bed.

"Maybe he'll find his horse," said Cora. The whirring of her flax wheel stopped. "What's wrong with you? You aren't lookin' too pert."

"I don't know exactly," said Mr. Thompson, stooped as an old man as he pulled off his boots. "Just tired, I reckon."

"You worked too hard cutting wood. A good night's rest and you'll perk right up," said Cora. She rose and crossed the cabin, showing Ellen and Willie to the loft ladder. "Up to the loft, Ellie. You, too, Willie. Settle in with the young'uns and get you some sleep."

The tenderness of her touch as she brushed a strand of hair from Ellen's face gave Ellen the same stir of unease that Father's precaution had. *Were the grown-ups keeping a secret from her and Willie? If so, what?*

Ellen fell asleep wondering.

Mr. Thompson had the shakes the next morning and wasn't well enough to crawl out of bed.

"Ague," said Mrs. Thompson, with a furrowed brow as she pulled the blanket up under Mr. Thompson's chin. "He gets it in the spring, just as regular as clockwork."

Ellen helped her fix breakfast for the little ones and cleaned up the dishes before walking home with Willie to do the chores.

They repeated the procedure when evening came, and again the next day. Mr. Thompson wasn't much improved the following morning, either. Ellen didn't need to consult her marked wall to know the significance of the day.

"Jack's thirty days are up," she told Willie as they ambled home to do morning chores.

"Think he'll be home today?"

"If not today, then soon," said Ellen. She crowded out thoughts of Indians and that powder keg Father had mentioned. "Father, too."

"Think they'll come together?"

"Maybe," said Ellen. "Father's debt to Mr. Iles is due. He needs to get to Springfield tomorrow."

Matilda was glad to see them. She strutted after Ellen and Willie as they fed the stock and milked the cow. They had been taking the milk back to the Thompson house where it wouldn't go to waste.

"You reckon Mrs. Thompson would miss us if we were to put the raft on the creek awhile?" asked Willie.

"I guess we wouldn't be shirking duty if we were to play for a spell," reasoned Ellen, who had worked at being a help to the Thompsons. "We can pick up the milk on our way back."

Ellen set the bucket of milk down in the spring where it would stay cool, then raced after Willie into the woods and to the nearby creek.

Wild plum trees and purple redbuds lined the creek in a flowering mist of white and purple. Ellen and Willie pushed the raft down the bank over a carpet of wildflowers and into the water.

"Where shall we go?" asked Willie.

"Louisa's," said Ellen, breathing the fragrance of wild plum.

"Pretend we see Indians on the way," said Willie.

Enjoying the freedom from household tasks, Ellen and Willie lost track of the time, and of Matilda, too. At length, they pulled the raft back up the bank. But they couldn't return to the Thompsons' without first closing Matilda in.

"Matilda! Matilda!" called Willie.

"Matilda!" chimed Ellen, trailing him along the winding creek bank. "Matil . . ."

A horse! Ellen caught a glimpse, and then another, as it picked its way through the woods. The rider's features were hidden by leaves and sprays of flowering trees. But the horse looked just like Gertie!

"Jack!" Shock fading, Ellen broke into a run as wild as her heartbeat. "Jack! Jack! It's us, Jack!"

But it wasn't Jack!

Ellen stopped so fast, Willie ran over her heels.

"Who is it?" whispered Willie, clutching her from behind.

A *stranger*. Bewhiskered, bedraggled. Tall and lean with a nose as blunt as a stump, he lost his hat as he dismounted. Ellen's nerves twitched at the sight of an angry, half-healed gash beneath the dark, dull hair feathering his brow.

"Howdy, young'uns," he called, and stooped to pick up his hat. "I'm looking for the Tandy place."

"Tandy? That's us," said Willie.

"No foolin'? Do you know a feller named Jack Tandy?"

"He's my brother!"

"Who are you?" said Ellen.

"Ishmael Robb. Didn't mean to startle you," he added as Ellen frowned a warning at Willie. "I'm a friend of Jack's."

"Jack?" Relief, hope, fear caught in Ellen's throat like tangled yarn and jerked hard on her heartstrings. "Where is he? Is he with you?"

"No, Sis. He's still waiting to be mustered out." The man thumbed up Willie's chin. "Well, looky here. If you ain't the spittin' image of Jack!"

Willie pushed out his chest and said, "I'm Willie, she's Ellie. If you're looking for Father, he's not here."

"He hasn't gone far, he'll be along directly," Ellen said quickly.

Mr. Robb flashed a stained and gappy grin. "Yer smart to be careful, Sis. But rest easy. I don't mean you no harm. Jack figur't the distaff side of the family would be frettin'. I promised him I'd look you up and let you know he's fit."

"He is?" cried Ellen, hands flying to her face. "He's all right, Willie! He's all right!"

Willie flung his arms around Ellen and jumped for joy. Ellen laughed and jumped, too. Wondering about Mr. Robb's limp, she let slide his use of "distaff," a word meant for Mama, and asked, "Is there something wrong with your foot?"

"Thigh injury," he said, gingerly patting his left leg. "Tangled with an Injun in the first wave of attack. Noggin's painin' me some, too."

"Attack? You fought Indians?" cried Willie.

"Shorely did. You didn't know there'd been fighting?"

"No!" cried Ellen, hair rising on her neck.

"Black Hawk and his injuns come apourin' out of that timber thick as hornets up north at Old Man's Creek. And us, down in a slough. Thunderation, we took a stingin'! Major Stillman hisself run, and the rest of us, too."

"When?"

"Been a week now."

Father must have known! It wasn't just to carry a message that he had gone. He had gone to see about Jack! Understanding now why he had been so quick to carry the courier's message, Ellen pressed closer. "You're sure Jack wasn't hurt?"

"He come through without a scratch. Not all of us was so lucky," the man added, and winced as he reached for the stirrup.

"You never did say how you came to have Gertie," said Ellen. Seeing him swing aboard Gertie jarred like that word "distaff."

"The horse, you mean? Mine got shot out from under me, so Jack let me borry it on account I had orders to take a message to the gov'nor. Reckon I best not keep him waiting," he added, and bid them good day.

Chapter Eighteen

Watching Mr. Robb disappear through the trees on Father's horse gave Ellen an uneasy stir that lingered as she and Willie trekked through the woods, looking for Matilda. By the time they finally found her, Willie was so relieved she hadn't become lunch for a wolf, he hardly scolded the goose at all.

"I'll close her in the barn, you get the milk," said Ellen as they neared home. When she had done so, she returned to the spring where Willie waited with the bucket of milk.

"Ready?"

Ellen nodded, then paused and asked, "Think we should take Mrs. Thompson some corn flour? Her supply is getting low, and Mr. Thompson's in no shape to go to the mill."

"All right. But hurry. I'm getting hungry."

Ellen raced to the cabin and lifted her foot for the stoop.

The stoop wasn't there! It had been pried away and flung to one side! The yawning door creaked open. All the air went out of Ellen's lungs. The furniture was overturned. Dishes and bedding and feathers and broken crocks were scattered everywhere. Part of the floor had been pried loose!

Ellen wheeled and shouted for Willie. He rounded the cabin from the west, and stopped in the open door. His face turned as white as the sloshing milk. He set the bucket down hard.

"Who did this?"

Ellen gripped her stomach, fighting the chilly spasms, thinking about Jack. About Mr. Robb. About distaff. "Distaff!" she said out loud.

"Huh?"

"Mr. Robb!"

"But he's Jack's friend!" protested Willie.

Was he? Or had he just told them what they wanted to hear?

"He was nice, Ellie," Willie argued. "He brought a message from Jack all this way just to keep us from worrying."

"To keep the *distaff* side of the family from worrying," Ellen stressed the word that had glared even as Mr. Robb spoke it. "That's Mama, Willie. Jack's friends know Mama's dead and that Julia's gone."

"Maybe he meant you," said Willie in a shrinking voice.

Ellen could see how badly he wanted to believe in Mr. Robb. Part of her wanted to believe, too. But the low simmer inside was heating to a rolling boil of doubt. *Two messengers passing through Tandy Grove all within a couple of days? How likely was that? But if he wasn't a friend, then why had he come? Where was Jack, really?* Ellen flung her hands over her eyes. It didn't stop the awful rush of dark possibilities.

"He wasn't carrying a message. And he wasn't here to set our minds at ease, either," said Ellen. "Oh, Willie! Don't you see! He lied! Jack didn't give him Father's horse, he took it!"

"From Jack?"

"Yes!"

"Then where's Jack?"

"I don't know," said Ellen, heat building behind her eyes. "But look at the place! He's torn it apart!"

"You don't know it was him," said Willie stubbornly.

"Who else is there?" she cried. "He's a thief, Willie! He stole Jack's horse and he was looking for something else to steal."

Father's gold! The words dropped into her mind, too horrible to speak. They had no other valuables. She raced to the fireplace, ducked inside, and looked for the loose stone in the chimney.

"Is it there?" cried Willie, crowding into the cold ashes.

Ellen dropped the stone. Her knees nearly buckled when her fingers touched the smoke-softened deerskin pouch. Thank God! She loosened the drawstring and plunged her hand past inside. The gold, wrapped in rags, was still there!

A shadow crossed the greased paper window. Ellen's heart jumped with sick certainty. With trembling fingers, she opened the pouch and poured the gold coins into the milk bucket.

Wide-eyed, Willie asked, "What'd you do that . . ."

She clamped a hand over his mouth, and whispered,

"We're going to Thompsons'. You carry the bucket. Go on! Pick it up!"

Willie's freckles stood out from his white face. But he walked out the door without looking back. Ellen was right behind him when she heard a horse sneeze. She hadn't imagined it. Robb *was* out there! *Use your head, Ellie. Use your head. Help me, God!*

Blood rushing, Ellen slipped Father's bull's tongue plowshares into the leather pouch. She crammed rags on top to disguise the shape, then tugged the drawstring tight.

"You coming?" Willie called to her from the woodpile on the north side of the cabin.

Certain Robb was lying in wait, Ellen called back, "Go to Louisa's, Willie."

"Louisa's?"

"Go on!" she cried, willing him to understand where she meant for him to hide. "I'll catch up in a second."

Ishmael Robb rode around the side of the cabin on Father's horse, Gertie, just as Ellen stepped into the sunshine.

"Mr. Robb!" blurted Ellen, pretending to be glad to see him. "Thank goodness! I just sent Willie for help! Somebody's broke into our cabin!"

Mr. Robb looked through the open door and whistled. "Boy, howdy, looks like a couple of Arkansas bears scampered through!"

"Can you help us, Mr. Robb? Would you ride to Pekin and get the sheriff?"

"What should I tell the sheriff they was lookin' for?"

"I don't know!" cried Ellen, thrusting the pouch behind her back with one hand, plucking her skirt with the other. "We've got nothing of value."

"You don't, eh? What's that you're sneaking behind yer back, Sis?" he growled and lurched at her from the saddle.

Ellen ducked and screamed and cowered against the cabin. Robb leaped out of the saddle and grabbed her. She wrenched free and swung the pouch, aiming at his head. But he deflected the blow with an upraised arm.

"No more games, Sis!" he snarled. "Hand over yer pa's gold now, before you git hurt."

Ellen dodged and ran, as if it were their life savings. But he caught her, snagged the pouch, and shoved her to the ground. "Set now, and stay set, you hear?" he warned.

The cold steel in his eyes sucked the breath from Ellen. She stayed where she was, heart pounding as he stuffed the pouch into his saddlebags and mounted up. Not until he rode south did she jump to her feet.

"Father'll catch you! He'll skin you alive! Nobody steals from us and gets away with it!" she shouted after him.

His hoofbeats faded in the distance.

How far would he go before he looked in the pouch? Ellen flew to the creek for Willie. He was crouched in the weeds near the raft.

"Where's the gold?"

Willie patted his bulging pockets and darted into the woods. "Come on, Ellie. Mr. Thompson'll help us!"

How could he when he was sick in bed? But what else could they do?

The answer dropped to mind in a wordless whisper. Ellen picked up the bucket of milk, her mind made up. "We're not going to Thompsons'."

"Where then?"

"To Springfield. We're taking the gold to Mr. Iles before something happens to it."

Willie's jaw dropped, a storm of protest in his eyes. "We can't, Ellie. It's too far!"

"Yes, we can!"

"How?" he demanded.

"Shh! I'm thinking."

Ellen studied the raft. But there was so much debris in the creek. They'd be blocked by logjams. Anyway, the Springfield-Fort Dearborn Road was the shortest route. *And the most dangerous should Robb check his saddlebags and turn back.*

Chapter Nineteen

Hungry, yet afraid to return to the house for provisions, Ellen and Willie drank from the milk bucket as they skirted the beaten track to Springfield. Willie worried about getting lost while Ellen worried about Jack and Father, and Mr. Robb turning back and bumping right into them.

One thing she knew for sure—Jack hadn't given up Father's horse willingly. Praying he was safe, Ellen trudged on through a mix of timber and prairie with Willie at her side. They stayed within sight of the road, but off of it so as to have time to duck for cover if need be.

But they saw no sign of Mr. Robb, or anyone else. They didn't even see any wildlife, either. No rabbits, no squirrels, no grouse, no deer. The animals had yet to recover from the killing Winter of the Deep Snow. They drank a lot of milk, and poured some on the ground, and still the wooden bucket was heavy.

In the middle of the afternoon, Willie begged for a rest. They stretched out on the ground in the shelter of some trees.

"Milk's turning to butter from all the jostling," said Willie.

"Soured, more'n likely," said Ellie. She tasted it, made a face, and dumped it. There was no point in hauling an empty bucket all the way to Springfield. Ellen hung it in a tree by the side of the road.

"We'll pick it up on the way home."

"If we can find it again," said Willie.

Ellen had him empty his pockets. She put the gold up her sunbonnet, knotted it, and tied the strings around her waist.

It was a long, anxious trail. Just before sunset, they stopped on the bank of a creek. Tired, footsore, and hungry, they got out from under the trees and searched the rolling prairie for chimney smoke to indicate a cabin, but found none.

"Guess we'll have to eat greens." Ellen stooped and picked some dock and dandelion leaves.

Willie wrinkled his nose. "Reckon we're halfway yet?"

"I don't think so," said Ellen. "We haven't crossed Salt Creek."

"That's halfway?"

"Close. We'll have to get up before daylight and set a good pace if we're going to reach Mr. Iles on time."

Ellen followed Willie into the woods again. She poked beneath a dead elm tree, looking for wild mushrooms. Had Father found Jack? Was he all right? Had they come home? Were they wondering right now what had become of her and Willie just as she was wondering where they were and if they were all right. *God knows*, Mama's words whispered in Ellen's memory.

"Will Mr. Iles be mad at Father if we're late?" Willie broke into her thoughts.

"I don't know," said Ellen. She did know money was hard to come by, and that few were willing to lend it. The loan showed that Mr. Iles trusted Father to be a man of his word. It was more than gold they were carrying, it was Father's reputation. Ellen spotted a mushroom nestled in undergrowth and stooped to pick it.

"Help me look, Willie."

"Raw mushrooms?"

"You want to eat, don't you? Here's another one."

Half hidden by mats of damp leaves, the morels were hard to see in the dwindling light. But Ellen had a nose for mushrooms. Jack always laughed when she said she could smell them, but she really could. By the time the light was gone from the sky, she had found a dozen and Willie had found wild onions. They washed their scanty meal in the creek by the light of the rising moon. It wasn't very tasty uncooked. But the weakness in Ellen's limbs went away when she had eaten.

They drank from the creek, then gathered dried leaves for a bed, and brush, more leaves, and bark for a covering. They piled it against a log and crawled beneath it.

"I think I ate a bug," said Willie, his back to the log.

Ellen had eaten them, too. It was hard to get the tiny ones out of the mushrooms. "It won't hurt you."

"Wish I had that milk to wash out the taste, though."

"It was sour."

"I wish I had milk that wasn't sour," he said.

Ellen wished for hoecakes and spit-roasted beef. She

wished for home and Father and Jack. She wished the mosquitoes would quit chewing on her. She heard a soft sound in the grass and wished for Silas and his snake-killing whip.

An owl hooted. Fireflies flitted. Something splashed in the nearby water.

"Hear that?" whispered Willie, rising on one elbow.

"Just a fish jumping."

Ellen's voice came out braver than she was feeling. Willie snuggled closer. His breath tickled her neck. His bony knees jabbed her back, but she didn't complain. Not even when he ground his teeth in his sleep.

Ellen awakened later to find the moon shining and wolves chorusing in stuttering barks. They sounded close. Too close. She held her breath beneath their pungent makeshift covers and heard undergrowth rustling beneath padding steps. Soft panting. Gleaming eyes, rank fur, damp tongue!

Ellen leaped screaming to her feet in an explosion of brush and leaves and bark. She crashed into Willie, stumbled over the log, rolled onto her stomach, covered her head with her hands, and tore the air with her shrieks.

"Wolf! It's Wolf! Ellie, it's Wolf," Willie shouted.

Wolf barked and yipped and wagged his tail and walked all over Ellen as the truth seeped through her paralyzed brain. But her relief was short-lived, for beneath Wolf's joyous yips was the sucking of hooves in mud. The jingle of reins. A horse snuffling, splashing across the creek.

Robb?

"Hello, the camp!"

Panic's second blast ended with a whimper as Willie leaped up, squealing, "Silas?"

"Willie?" Silas stumbled up the bank, leading a horse. "What are you *doing* here?"

"What are *you* doing here?"

"I'm off to fight Indians," said Silas. "Least I was thinking about it. What about you?"

"We're taking Father's gold to Mr. Iles in Springfield," said Willie. "Trying to, anyway. It was Ellie's idea," he added, faintly accusing.

"What's he talking about?" asked Silas, turning to Ellen.

Ellen explained as best she could. Silas didn't interrupt or scoff over her fear of being overtaken by Robb. When she fell silent, he stroked his chin and said, "I guess I can be a soldier another time. You want to sleep or ride?"

"Ride," said Ellen. "We're short on time. The loan's due tomorrow."

"We'll make it," said Silas. He nudged Ellen then, and asked, "Was that you, caterwauling? Sounded like a cougar screaming."

"You're a good one to talk, squalling over a puny scoldin' from Father," muttered Ellen.

"What about you, standing there bawling and not once saying if I hadn't whipped you on purpose?"

"I did so say it!"

"When?" Silas shot back. "I didn't hear you."

"'Course you didn't. You were in the cowshed."

"What'd Father say?"

"He said you shouldn't have done it at all."

Silas shuffled his feet and admitted, "It *was* pretty stupid."

"So's making such a fuss over a little yellin'," said Ellen. "Why, if Willie and Jack and me screamed and rolled for cover every time Father raised his voice, we'd have packed down the ground till nothin'd grow!"

"How was I supposed to know it was just going to be yelling?"

"What else would it be?"

"Nothing. I'm done talking about it, so shut up or you can walk to Springfield!"

Ellen wondered about Julia, and what had happened to make Silas run away, and if he'd really been going to fight Indians, or if maybe he was . . .

"You were coming home, weren't you!" she blurted.

"Was not."

"You were so! You called Father, *Father*!"

"Did not."

"Did so!"

"That's it! You're walking," said Silas. "Come on, Willie. Let's leave her for the wolves."

"Hold the horse," said Ellen, not a bit worried. "I'm riding in front."

For once, Silas didn't argue. He gave her a leg up, scrambled on after her, and pulled Willie up behind him. Ellen soon wished she'd gotten a drink first. Her throat hurt from screaming at terrors that weren't even real. They'd seemed real at the time, though.

Maybe Silas's had, too, all those months ago.

Chapter Twenty

Ellen and the boys reached Springfield by mid-afternoon. Folks on foot and horseback picked their way down rutted streets, bustling about their business. It was more homes and stores and people than Ellen had ever seen all in one spot. Maybe when they had finished Father's business, they could browse awhile.

"Whoa. Right here," said Silas. He pointed through a propped open door beyond a board walkway. "That's Mr. Iles behind the desk."

The stout building had windows of real glass and a floor sanded so smooth you couldn't tell where one board ended and another began. Father's merchant-turned-banker friend had a prosperous bearing in his store-bought suit and white shirt. His high collar looked even stiffer than Ellen's poor aching muscles. Feeling dirty and dowdy, she slid to the ground, stamped the needles from her tired feet, and entreated Silas with an upward glance.

"Are you coming in with us?"

"Better not. I suppose Mother's got me torn by wolves or drowned by now. I'll go home and take my licking."

"Come on then, Willie," said Ellen.

"Can't I go with Silas and help him take his licking?"

"Julia isn't going to whip him," said Ellen, though in truth, she would take one herself just to see Julia again. But Julia might not feel the same way. "Climb down, Willie. I'm not facing that banker man all by myself."

Willie's face fell. But he dropped to the ground beside her. Ellen combed her fingers through her tangled hair. With a wistful glance at Silas and Wolf, she turned and walked inside with Willie.

The scratch of quill on ledger stopped as they approached the banker's desk. He lifted his head. "Who have we here?"

"I'm Ellen Tandy. This is my brother, Willie. You're Mr. Iles?"

"Yes, I am," he said, leaning back in his chair.

"Father sent us," said Ellen, too worn out to go into the whole tale. She untied her sunbonnet from around her waist and dropped it on the desk with a thud.

Mr. Iles stroked his lip and looked from her to the bonnet and back again before his face cleared. "You must be Gil Tandy's youngsters."

"Yes. You can count it if you want to," added Ellen.

"Your older brother waiting outside, is he?"

"He went on down the street," said Ellen, even though she knew he meant Jack, not Silas.

"There for a minute, I thought you'd come by yourselves. But that'd be more than any man would expect of children. Even Gil."

"Yup," said Willie, taking his cues from Ellen.

Mr. Iles smiled and asked about Father and how

they'd weathered the harsh winter before counting the gold. A burden lifted from Ellen as he dipped his quill in the ink pot, scribbled a receipt, and walked them to the door with words of good will for Father.

Ellen's thoughts turned to Julia as she followed Willie into the sunshine. Why hadn't she asked Silas where he and Julia were staying?

"Is that . . . Look, Ellie!" cried Willie.

"Ellie! Willie!" Julia's mouth jerked as she flew up the street. Her leghorn hat flopped over her day cap as she ran to them with open arms. "I knew the minute I heard the call for volunteers that Jack would go. But I never dreamed Gil would leave you two alone!"

"He didn't," said Ellen, startled by her tears. "He left us with the Thompsons. But Mr. Thompson got sick. Then Mr. Robb tried to steal the gold, and we were afraid if we didn't . . ."

The rest of her explanation was snuffed out by Julia's embrace. Her tears fell on Ellen like rain on cracked ground. They took the sting from her sunburn, the ache from her limbs, and the itch from her bug bites, and washed away forever her fear that Julia had stopped caring about them.

Ellen didn't notice much about the town or the stores they passed as they walked to the one-room home behind Julia's hat shop. Julia stuffed her and Willie and Silas full of soup and corn dodgers and listened as they told her all that had happened since Father had left with the message for General Atkinson.

Afterward, Julia heated water and sent the boys

out to play while Ellen bathed in the washtub and dressed in Julia's muslin night shift. The neck was too big and the arms too long and the skirt pooled around her feet. But it smelled nice. It smelled like Julia. And it was comforting. Like the worn quilt covering the bed, the feather tick, and Julia's voice as she tucked her in. Ellen closed her eyes and faded into the softness.

Was she dreaming, or was someone pounding on the door? The voice was Father's. Julia's bare feet whispered across the floor. The bolt creaked free.

"Sorry to bother you in the middle of the night, Julia . . ."

"It's all right. Ellen and Willie are here."

"Thank God! Are they all right?"

"Yes. They're sleeping."

Too drowsy to remember what it was she'd gone to bed feeling anxious over, Ellen snuggled deeper into her quilts and tried to tuck the voices into the fabric of a fading dream.

"What got into them, taking off like that?"

"They came to pay off your note to Mr. Iles."

"With what?"

"With the gold."

"You mean *they* took it? I thought sure Robb stole it."

"You know about him, then?"

"Oh, yes, I've got him all figured out."

"Are you coming in, Mr. Tandy?"

Father made a gruff sound, like rust on plowshares.

Ellen kept her eyes closed as his ringing steps approached the bed.

"Ellen?" Father touched her shoulder. "Sit up here. Or don't you want to hear about Jack?"

Jack? Ellen bolted upright in bed. "You saw Jack?"

"Up north," said Father. "He's expecting to be mustered out in a few days."

"He's all right?"

"Yes. He's fine."

All at once, Ellen felt so light and good, anything seemed possible. Including having a mother again. She caught Father's hand. "Silas rescued us, Father. If it wasn't for him, no telling where we'd be."

"Silas?" Father asked in surprise.

"He was coming home and he found us on the way and brought us to town with the gold. See, Mr. Robb tried to steal it, only we tricked him and he stole your plowshares instead."

"My plowshares?"

In the flickering firelight, Ellen saw his brows draw together and wished she'd saved that part for later. "Sorry," she mumbled, and dropped his hand.

"I didn't mean . . ." Father glanced at Julia, then raked his hand over his face. When he spoke again, the gruffness was gone from his voice. "Go on, Ellen."

"I'll tell you," Julia spoke up. "Let her go back to sleep."

Ellen was about to protest that she was too wide awake now. Then she saw Julia looking at Father and Father looking back, and decided maybe it was a good time to be tired after all. She yawned and closed her eyes, and snuggled into her pillow as if her ears were closed, too.

"Would you like some tea, Mr. Tandy?"

Father declined the offer, and crossed to the slat bed where Willie and Silas slept.

"I take it you got the courier's message to the general?" said Julia, following.

"He wasn't a courier and it wasn't a real message. It was Robb, scheming to send me off to tall timber so he'd have easy pickin's. Misbegotten coward."

"I can't say I'm surprised. People know who you are and what you do, and that it takes capital."

"It was more than guesswork. It was Jack's careless words brought Robb to our door."

"Jack?" said Julia.

"Robb was in Jack's company. He overheard Jack mention the gold. When Robb stole his horse and deserted, Jack got a bad feeling about where he was headed, and reported him to General Atkinson."

"I thought General Atkinson was with the regular army."

"He is. But by that time, the regular army had caught up with the volunteers. Jack knew the general from taking cattle to Fort Armstrong, and was worried enough to ask him if he'd send word down to us to be on the lookout for Robb."

"It must have scared you when you realized what he was up to!"

"Mostly, I was kicking myself for being taken in.

Figured if I was that big a fool, I deserved to get robbed," said Father. His voice dropped, as if he'd remembered the sleeping children. "I didn't once think about Ellen and Willie getting caught up in it. They were supposed to be at Jeb and Cora's place. Then I got home and the place was in shambles . . . I don't know what got into Jack, telling our personal business that way."

"He was just talking, the way boys will."

"He knows better!" Father was spitting gravel again.

"I'm sure he does. But Mr. Robb must be very cunning. After all, he deceived you," added Julia.

"He wouldn't have, if I hadn't been worried over Jack."

"You're entitled to a mistake now and then, Mr. Tandy."

"Me?"

"Yes, you."

"I'm not looking for a quarrel," growled Father. "I'll just wake Willie and we'll start on home."

"Willie and Ellen aren't going anywhere. Not tonight," said Julia firmly, and straight away, began telling him about Robb first approaching the children in the woods. She continued uninterrupted to the moment Ellen had dropped the gold in the milk bucket and tricked Robb with the plowshares before setting off to Springfield with Willie.

Father inserted a grunt of approval, then shared how the milk bucket left in the tree had told him that he was on their trail. "I couldn't think why Willie and Ellie would have the milk bucket. But it was just like something Ellie would do, putting it in the tree for safe-keeping. All I could figure out was they must be going to Clarissa's. When I didn't find them there, you were my last hope."

"I take it Mr. Robb hasn't been caught?"

"Not yet, he hasn't. Don't suppose there's much chance of getting Gertie back, or my plowshares, either. Though I guess that is a small price compared to Ellie and Willie risking life and limb."

"You look tired. When did you last sleep?"

"Been a spell," Father admitted.

"I'll get some quilts and make a bed for you in the shop."

"I won't be in your way?"

"No, of course not," said Julia. "Unless you'd rather go."

"Do you want me to go?"

"Gil, I just said . . ."

"I heard what you said. But I can't hear what you're not saying. Last time we talked . . ."

"We didn't talk, we shouted, and still neither of us heard what the other one was saying," said Julia. "That was my mistake. I've made several."

"Such as?"

"Marrying you for the wrong reasons."

"What would the right reason have been?"

"Because I wanted to," said Julia. "Instead, it was fear. Fear we couldn't survive on our own on the frontier. I did what I thought I had to do."

"You didn't get that idea from me."

"Gil Tandy, you are too looking for a quarrel."

"No, I'm not. I came looking for my family. All of it." Father's voice dropped as he added, "Or is it too late for that?"

"I thought it was. I was wrong."

"About that day," Father began. "I've been all these months thinking about it, and how Silas went to pieces when I hadn't laid a hand on him."

"He hadn't been struck since his father died. It was the fear of it starting all over again," said Julia quietly.

"He's been treated rough, then?"

Ellen didn't hear Julia's reply. All she heard was Father pressing her, asking, "What about you? Was he rough with you, too?"

"It doesn't matter about me. Silas . . ."

"It matters to me," Father cut in. "Why didn't you tell me from the start?"

"I couldn't." Voice knotting, Julia murmured, "He wasn't always that way. There were good times, too. Though fewer, as the years went by. And the damage to Silas . . ." Julia stopped.

"You should have told me."

"I wanted to bury it with him. I still do," murmured Julia.

"You can't. Not unless you bury yourself and the boy, too."

"It's hard to talk about."

"It's hard to listen to," countered Father. "But I mean to."

"All right, Gil. But not here. For now, I just want to

say that I was wrong about what Silas needs from you."

"What does he need?" asked Father.

"The same thing Ellen and Willie and Jack need. And get." Julia opened the door into the adjoining shop. "Though it could be tempered with a good deal more patience."

Ellen had heard more than she wanted to. She was glad when the door closed behind them. *How rough was rough?* Rough enough that it was wrong to Father, and he was no milksop. It cut her to think of anyone being rough with Julia. Or with Silas, despite his irritating ways.

After a while, Julia returned alone. "Julia?" whispered Ellen, making room for her in the bed. "Are you coming home with us?"

"Yes," said Julia.

"I'm glad."

"Me, too." Julia's arms closed around Ellen.

"Are we stopping at Aunt Clarissa's?" she asked, snuggling close.

"We are. We're going to spend several days with them."

"Father agreed? I can't wait!"

"Then go to sleep and let it be morning," said Julia.

Ellen tried. But her mind raced with all the things she had to tell Louisa. They had so much catching up to do! Would there be time to work on Aunt Clarissa's Orange Peel quilt?

Ellen fingered the border of the quilt tucked snugly around her and Julia. It was an old quilt. The fabric was worn. In places, frayed stitches exposed threads and raw seams. But overall it was well stitched. It would hold together for some time. That's what she wanted.

Not a perfect family, but a family pieced together with love. A family that stayed together, even when the raw edges showed.

Epilogue

"And it did," said Lacey.

"Yes, it did." Gram smiled and rose from the quilting frame to stretch the kinks from her shoulders. She said, "Eight children were born to Julia and Gil, which made twelve in all, counting Silas. He changed his name to Tandy, remember."

"Did Gil quit yelling at him? Or did he just get used to it?" asked Ellen.

"Some of both, I suppose. Learning the difference between respect and fear probably helped, too," said Gram. "There were struggles, I'm sure. That's how families are made. One stitch at a time."

"Even our family?"

"Yes, indeed," said Gram.

Cloth from different bolts. Lacey thought again of Silas changing his name. "Gram? If Silas *hadn't* changed his name, then Grampa Max's name would have been Max Pierce, and your name would be Pierce, and Dad's name would be Pierce, and . . . Gram! I just now realized! My name would be Pierce, too!"

"That's right," said Gram. "You're a Tandy by blood through my family and a Tandy by name through Max's, going back to Silas."

Gram's husband, Grampa Max, had died before

Lacey was born. She asked, "Is that why you married Grampa? To get back the Tandy name?"

"That and his handsome smile," said Gram, a twinkle in her eye.

Lacey crossed to the window. She wished she could see back across the years to the days when Ellen and Silas and Willie had built their raft on the creek and Ellen had learned to quilt, and oh! so many things!

"Gram? Could we make a quilt?"

"Certainly. How about a sunbonnet quilt?" asked Gram.

"Sunbonnet girls! Of course! I'll pretend one sunbonnet girl is Ellie. She'll be blue. Julia should be, too, since that was her favorite color. Louisa can be red to match her hair, don't you think?"

"You aren't going to leave the boys out, are you?"

Lacey giggled at the idea of boys in bonnets.

"We'll dress them in straw hats and bib overalls," said Gram. "I have the pattern for that, too. I believe it is called Overall Boys."

"Then I can make a square for every family hero!"

"Now that *is* ambitious!" But Gram's eyes shone as the idea took root.

Hearing a car, Lacey looked out the window again. "Shoot. Judith's back. I guess we can't start today."

"We already have. Quilts begin up here." Gram tapped her temple.

Sheri darted up the walk, a basketball under her arm. Ivana, dressed in cotton-candy pink, was huddled beneath her umbrella. Lacey stayed at the window as

Gram crossed to the door to meet them.

"Don't bounce that ball in the house, Sheri. Ivana, you're dripping. Leave the umbrella at the door. I'm sorry we're late, Jenny," Judith apologized to Gram as she wiped her feet.

"You're not late, you're just in time for tea. How was your piano lesson, Ivana?"

"Fine, thanks," Ivana said, dimpling.

"A little more practice and she'll be ready for her recital," said Judith. She called to Lacey. "What have you and Gram been doing?"

"Telling stories," Gram answered for her.

"About a raft and a flood and a bunch of other stuff. Abe Lincoln was in it, too. Wasn't he, Gram?" Lacey said, turning away from the window.

"Lincoln! I'm doing a report on his New Salem days for school," said Ivana.

"Too bad you missed it," said Lacey.

"You can tell her about it while I put the kettle on," said Gram. "Cookies, anyone?"

"None for me, Jennie. I'm watching my weight," said Judith. "But tea sounds wonderful."

"Girls?"

"Cookies with milk, please," said Ivana.

"Just cookies, please," Sheri said, stashing her ball in the firewood box by the door.

Gram crooked an eyebrow at Lacey, but it wasn't a question about cookies or the memory quilt. Lacey looked at her stepsisters and then at Gram. It had been a great morning. But there were things Gram couldn't do that sisters could. *If you overlooked the raw edges.* Lacey took a deep breath, then crossed the room and retrieved Sheri's basketball from the firewood box.

"Hey!" yelped Sheri. "Where're you going with that?"

"The barn," said Lacey. "There's a basketball hoop in the hayloft."

"There is? Wait'll I grab some cookies," said Sheri.

"We can look for wood scraps while we're there. For our raft," added Lacey.

"You have a raft?" asked Sheri.

"I was thinking we could build one."

"And float it on the creek? Cool!" Sheri said, quickening her step. "Hey, Ivana! Me and Lacey are going to build a raft. You want to help?"

✸ AMERICAN QUILTS SERIES ✸
Activity Pages by Stasia Kehoe
April 13, 2000

BOOK 1: ELLEN's STORY

Make a Memory: Heirloom Pictures

Quilts help Lacey's grandmother remember important moments of family history. The quilts have become family heirlooms. Family heirlooms do not have to be quilts.   Does your family have an old teapot, silver spoons, war medals, furniture, dolls, toys, or other special mementos from the past? Preserve the memories that go with these objects by making an heirloom picture. You will need:

A camera and film

White paper (acid-free if possible)

A smear-resistant calligraphy or scrapbook pen

Ellen's Story

A picture frame (8" X 10" or larger), available at most craft stores.

A glue stick (acid-free if possible)

Lace doilies, wrapping paper scraps, and/or other craft paper

Pinking or deckle shears (fancy edge-trimming scissors)

A satin or velvet ribbon about 48" long

Have an adult help you arrange and photograph your family heirloom(s). Have the pictures developed, then ask a parent or older relative about the item(s) you have photographed. Using the white paper and pen, write a short story about your family heirloom(s) and create labels for the photographs. If desired, trim your pictures, story, and/or labels with shears. Next, remove the back from the frame. Use the cardboard frame insert as the base for your picture. Create a background using the doilies and/or paper scraps. Arrange your photographs, story, and labels on top. Stick everything together with the glue stick. Other small flat objects, such as dried flowers, can also be attached. Carefully put your picture inside the frame and reseal the back. Use the ribbon to decorate the frame: Glue one large bow at the top center, or smaller bows in each corner of the frame. Hang your heirloom picture in a special place.

Quilting Corner: Name that Pattern

Traditional quilts are made up of patterned squares sewn together. Many quilts are named for import life events, familiar objects, or images from nature. Look through *Ellen's Story* to find descriptions of Julia's red quilt. Julia calls her quilt "Robbing Peter to Pay Paul." Later in the story, Aunt Clarissa calls a quilt of the same pattern "Orange Peel." Can you explain how each name describes the quilt pattern in a different way? Take a look at some books about quilting in your local library. Make a list of your favorite quilt patterns and their names. Then, try designing your own quilt. Use a ruler to divide a sheet of white drawing paper into nine equal squares. Sketch the quilt pattern in pencil on the squares, then add color with felt tip pens or colored pencils. Give your quilt pattern a descriptive name. Can you think of a second name that describes your pattern in another way? Show your design to a family member or friend, and ask what he or she would call your quilt.

School Stories: Frontier Classroom

Ellen doesn't go to school. Her mother taught her to read a little from the Bible. Later in the story, Julia teaches Ellen. Imagine studying in the same room in which you eat, sleep, and play, with just one book to read, and lessons taught only when someone had the time. Try being a frontier teacher yourself. Invite your sisters, brothers, or friends for a lesson in the kitchen. Use one book. Practice writing using sticks dipped in ink made from a bowl of crushed blueberries or blackberries. Do you and your "students" think this was a good way to learn? Why or why not? What might frontier children have understood better than today's kids? What things would frontier classrooms probably not teach as well as modern schools?

Family Tree Time: Three Generations

Lacey Tandy loves to learn about her great-great-great-great-grandparents and other relatives who lived long ago. Their very names spark her imagination. It is fascinating to find out about your family tree. Compile your own family tree. Start by finding out the names of all of your grandparents, aunts, uncles, and cousins. Then, at the top of a large sheet of paper, write the names of your grandparents. Move down a line for your parents, aunts, uncles, and their spouses. Move down one more line for you, your brothers, sisters, and cousins. The fun doesn't end with just three generations. Ask your local librarian or media specialist how to do more research on your family tree. See how far back you can go in history!

Presenting the Past: Native Americans

As American pioneers pushed westward toward California, they encountered many Native American peoples living on the land. Relations with Native American tribes were sometimes peaceful, sometimes conflicted. Go to the library or on-line to learn about America's early residents, their great diversity of tribes, and the ways of life that they were forced to change as the West became home to the new settlers.

American Quilt Questions: Blended Families

In *Ellen's Story*, we learn that Lacey and Ellen both become members of blended families. They live with their birth fathers, new mothers, and new siblings.

Do you think the reasons why Ellen's father married Julia were the same as the reasons Lacey's father married Judith? Explain.

Why is Judith so protective of Silas? Why do you think Silas cracks his father's whip all the time?

Do you think Ellen will grow to think of Willie, Jack, and Silas as brothers in the same way—and feel the same about them? Is this okay?

What upsets Ellen about the name of Julia's quilt, "Robbing Peter to Pay Paul"? Do you think this feeling troubles members of all blended families? Should it?

In what ways do you think blended families from the 19th and 21st centuries are probably the same? In what ways are blended families from the past and present probably different?

Gram tells Lacey: "Like quilts, families are pieced together over time." How does this sentence have special meaning for a blended family?

✸ **AMERICAN QUILTS SERIES** ✸

BOOK 2: HATTIE's STORY

Freckled, green-eyed Hattie McDaniels was a live spark
in a colony of dwindled dreams called Mount Hope.
She shook her dark hair and stamped her foot so hard
the ground shook. The covered wagon rolled away, taking her friend, Dora June Carlin, and the new teacher,
Miss Garnet, off to Kansas Territory.

"Stop! Come back, come back!" cried Hattie, running along behind.

The wheels turned. The words shifted and changed
into low voices and shuffling feet. The wagon melted
away, leaving only a moonlit room. Hattie rolled over in
bed and rubbed her eyes.

Sweet briar arched over the open window. A light
breeze breathed its apple-scented fragrance over Hattie's
quilt. She smelled meat frying in the next room. But it
felt like the dead of night

Hattie turned on her corn-husk mattress and slept

until birds sang and the sky brightened. She dressed and straightened the quilt. It was a repeating tulip pattern, and colorful. The center petals were coffin shaped. Their stems made black crosses.

Hattie didn't recall Mama piecing the quilt top. But she did remember helping quilt it. Two winters past, Poppa had altered the quilting frame to go over the bed after Dr. Proctor had said that Mama's only hope of delivering her baby safely was to stay off her feet. The baby came too early anyway. Mama was better at finishing quilts than finishing babies.

The door separating Hattie's room from the front room creaked as she opened it. She trotted over to the stone hearth and snuggled up to Mama. Short and round and warm and steamy, Mama was best this way, before the day scratched at that quick impatience that lay just below the surface.

"I love you, Mama."

"Sweetness, so early in the morning?" There was wood smoke in Mama's hug, in her hair, and in the crush of her calico dress. A scar left by the lash of a whip in childhood play seamed the soot-smudged cheek Hattie kissed.

"Where's Poppa? Has he eaten already?" asked Hattie.

"No, you're up just right. The porridge will be ready in a minute."

"Porridge?" Hattie tilted her turned-up nose. "I thought I smelled meat for breakfast."

"Not unless a frog stuck his toe in the pot when I was looking the other way."

Hattie giggled. "I must have dreamed it. I had some gummers."

"Gummers, eh?"

Hattie nodded and told Mama about her dream with Miss Garnet becoming Dora June's mama through marriage.

"It was Poppa talking about Kansas that made me dream it," finished Hattie. "Miss Garnet wouldn't really marry the constable. He's homely as homely can be."

"You better not let Dora June hear you say that. You're liable to hurt her feelings," cautioned Mama.

It would, sure enough. Mr. Carlin was a widower. His sister had come up from Kentucky to keep the cabin and look after Dora June. Dora June tolerated Auntie Carlin well enough. But she was flat-out devoted to her long-whiskered pa.

Mama gave the pot another stir, then crossed to one side of the fireplace for a skillet. Pegs, driven into the wall, held her collection of iron pots and kettles and pans. Hattie donned an apron and pulled the dining table out from the wall. She lifted one leaf and took the blue-edged dishes from the walnut cupboard.

"I'll finish. Go feed the chickens and gather the eggs," said Mama.

The path to the privy lead past the smokehouse, woodshed, and the freshly turned garden. Dew tickled and squashed between Hattie's toes. She tucked eggs into her apron pocket and turned the hens into the chicken yard with Hambone and her nine piglets. Poppa had already filled Hambone's trough. The little pigs were eating, too. The smallest of the litter, Wee Willie, saw Hattie and came running.

He chased the cracked corn she threw to the chicken, then trotted underfoot as she gathered the eggs into her apron pocket. Hattie climbed the fence and was on her way back to the house when Dora June and her pa came riding into Mount Hope at full gallop.

Constable Carlin stopped his horse at the front gate. "Is your pa around?" he called.

"He's in the barn," said Hattie. "Climb down, Dora June."

"Can I, Pa?" asked Dora June.

Mr. Carlin shifted his dippings from one jaw to the other. "I reckon," he said. "But don't wander off. This won't take long."

Mr. Carlin's long beard billowed as he swung down after Dora June. He tied his sweaty horse to the fence and skirted the enclosed yard.

"We had riders in the night, lookin' for runaways."

Hattie's heart jumped. "Slave hunters? Did they find them?"

"Shh!" Dora June flung a look after her father. "Pa doesn't know I was listening."

"But did they find them?"

"Not yet. The slave hunters ate breakfast with us. Auntie was making up beds for them when I left so's they can rest a spell. They been riding all night." Dora June nodded and combed her fingers through her pale wind-torn hair.

"So now what?"

"Pa's asking around the neighborhood for them, and trying to put together a search party. He has to, it's his job."

Illinois was a free state. But powerful pro-slavery men had hollered so about runaways escaping north that awhile back they passed a law that allowed slave hunters to search for runaways in free states too. Poppa said it was an unjust law. It would do no good to tell Dora June that. Already, she had her chin in the air the way she did each time they got close to what was a thin-ice subject.

"We passed Miss Garnet comin'." Dora June turned toward the road and added, "See? She's wearing blue today."

Hattie watched the schoolmarm, Miss Garnet, turn the corner into Mount Hope. She was staying the week on the Jennings farm several miles north of Mount Hope. Her snug-fitting jacket and skirt matched her blue eyes. Wisps of golden curl and a poke bonnet framed her face.

"Do you want some walk-along company?" Dora June called to her.

"Not this morning, Dora June," replied Miss Garnet, touching the white frills at her throat. "I have papers to mark and some sweeping up to do."

"Teachers have to sweep up?" Dora June sighed as Miss Garnet went on her way. "And here I was set on bein' one."

"Me, too." Hattie twisted a dandelion stem about her finger. "Isn't she just the prettiest lady you ever did see?"

"Stylish, too," said Dora June. "See how her skirt pouffes in back? You reckon it's all her?"

"I don't know. She's trim everywhere else."

"Puts a swing-swang to her walk." Dora June swung forward, hands tilted, cocked fingers and fluttering like little chicks. "Swing-swang, swing-swang," she chanted. "Swing-swang with me, Hattie!"

Hattie linked arms with Dora June. They circled the house, bottoms wagging, then collapsed giggling in the grass. Raised voices brought Hattie to her feet again.

"How'd you like it if somebody made off with your horses and you had no way of working your fields?" demanded Constable Carlin as he strode out of the barn after Poppa.

"It isn't the same thing," said Poppa.

"Shore, it is. Property's property. You buy it, you don't want it stolen away."

"Property *is* property," agreed Poppa. "People aren't."

"I ain't goin' to argie with you. The law compels you to help me look."

"I answer to a Higher law, Mr. Carlin."

"That's your last word?"

Poppa's long square-jawed face flared back a wordless answer.

Mr. Carlin jerked his hand at Dora June from the other side of the fence. She circled around front and bolted out the gate and up behind him without a word to Hattie.

"If I catch wind you know more than you're ownin' up to, I'll be back. I'll go the whole hog, searching this place." Short in the saddle and stout as stump, Mr. Carlin shifted his dancing horse and spat his cud of chewing tobacco.

It splatted at Poppa's feet. Poppa didn't budge. His gaze never faltered. But his color flared like wood dust flung on hot coals.

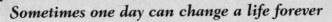

Sometimes one day can change a life forever

American Diaries

**Different girls,
living in different periods of America's past,
reveal their hearts' secrets in the pages
of their diaries. Each one faces a challenge
that will change her life forever.
Don't miss any of their stories:**